T0265946

# OUR TWELVE
# TRADITIONS

———— ◆ ————

AA members share their own
stories of experience

# OUR TWELVE
# TRADITIONS

———— ◆ ————

AA members share their own
stories of experience

**AAGRAPEVINE**,Inc.

New York, New York
WWW. AAGRAPEVINE.ORG

# AA PREAMBLE

Alcoholics Anonymous is a fellowship of men and women
who share their experience, strength and hope
with each other that they may solve their common problem
and help others to recover from alcoholism.

The only requirement for membership is a desire to stop drinking.
There are no dues or fees for AA membership;
we are self-supporting through our own contributions.
AA is not allied with any sect, denomination, politics, organization
or institution; does not wish to engage in any controversy,
neither endorses nor opposes any causes.

Our primary purpose is to stay sober
and help other alcoholics to achieve sobriety.

*©AA Grapevine, Inc.*

# Contents

**TRADITION ONE**

For the individual to recover, the group and the Fellowship must stick together

## TRADITION TWO
The only power and authority to be found in AA stems
from the group conscience

## TRADITION THREE
We're members of AA when we say we are—there is no
other qualification

## TRADITION FOUR
Wherever two or more alcoholics are gathered to practice
AA principles, they can call themselves a group

## TRADITION FIVE
No matter how different we may be, we are bound
by one common goal

## TRADITION SIX
Entanglements can overwhelm our purpose and
keep us from carrying the message

## TRADITION SEVEN
The spirit of responsibility defines our attitude toward money

## TRADITION EIGHT

While AA's Twelfth Step is never to be paid for, special workers can help make our Twelfth Step work possible

## TRADITION NINE

Finding the sweet spot between disorganization and getting things done

## TRADITION TEN

Steering clear of outside issues allows us to focus on what we do best

## TRADITION ELEVEN

Providing an example of sobriety can be more
powerful than promoting AA

## TRADITION TWELVE

Sacrifice is the watchword of anonymity

# WELCOME

"For thousands of alcoholics yet to come, A.A. does have an answer. But there is one condition. We must, at all costs, preserve our essential unity; it must be made unbreakably secure. Without permanent unity there can be little lasting recovery for anyone. Hence our future absolutely depends upon the creation and observance of a sound group Tradition."
—AA co-founder Bill W., *AA Grapevine*, October, 1947

Founded in 1935, AA's first decade was filled with an array of challenges and with little or no experience to hold onto, AA groups were often flying blind. Rules were made and broken; policies were introduced and soon discarded; and, inevitably, powerful, sometimes bitter, disputes broke out.

But AA was working—alcoholics were getting and staying sober—and soon the growing body of experience from the Fellowship's pioneering time began to crystallize into a set of working principles that could guide and protect the group life of AA.

In 1946, these core principles were codified by the founders and early members as the Twelve Traditions of Alcoholics Anonymous and were published in the April 1946 Grapevine under the title "Twelve Points to Assure Our Future." Wrote Bill W., AA's co-founder, "Nobody invented Alcoholics Anonymous. It grew. Trial and error has produced a rich experience. Little by little we have been adopting the lessons of that experience, first as policy and then as tradition. That process still goes on and we hope it never stops."

Since then, AA members have had years of experience with the principles outlined in the Twelve Traditions and as the stories in this collection show, those principles remain at the heart of Alcoholics Anonymous, providing ongoing guidance and protection for individuals, groups and the Fellowship as a whole.

Accepted and endorsed by the membership at AA's International Convention in Cleveland, Ohio, in 1950, application of the Traditions continues evolving today, and the stories here share the diverse experience, strength and hope of individual AA members and groups who have found workable solutions to difficult problems through these twelve vital principles.

Based on immutable values such as humility, responsibility, sacrifice and love, the Twelve Traditions provide the spiritual—and practical—underpinning for AA's ongoing adventure of living and working together. Our hope for this collection of stories, gathered from the broad experience of individual AAs, is that it will provide a pathway for members and groups to learn more about how these vital principles can be applied in our daily life.

# TRADITION ONE

Our common welfare should come first; personal
recovery depends upon A.A. unity.

———————◆———————

*For the individual to recover, the group and the Fellowship
must stick together.*

N ot especially known as "joiners" in our drinking days, "We alcoholics see," says Bill W., in the first appendix of the Big Book,
"that we must work together and hang together, else most of us
will finally die alone."

Warped by years of self-centeredness, this is difficult for many of
us to grasp at first. "The concept of a 'common welfare' was totally
alien to me," writes Kathleen D. in this chapter's story "A Thousand
Angels." "To be expected to put the needs of others in front of my own
was almost laughable," she writes. Yet, motivated by desperation, she
reached out. "I made a decision to accept this Tradition the same way
I accepted the truth of the First Step, not because I fully understood all
the implications and recognized their validity, but because I was desperate and I believed these were the only things that could save me."

Crossing the threshold into AA brings a deep satisfaction for
many of us, and the knowledge that at last, we belong.

"I began to get a glimmer of the miraculous promises available to
me by putting common welfare first," says Ed C. of Bowling Green,
Kentucky, in the article "Only Natural." "Instead of feeling diminished by being only a small part, I began to feel like I'd found a
home, a place where I belonged after a lifetime of isolation and being
fatally unique."

# A Thousand Angels

January 2014

When I first got to AA, I did not have any understanding of what the Steps could do for me, or how critical the Traditions are for the life of the group. But I knew in my heart that I needed meetings desperately. I knew that I was living from meeting to meeting the same way I had lived from bottle to bottle.

The First Tradition was a difficult concept for me. Having grown up in an alcoholic household, I learned never to trust anyone, never to let anyone see that I was scared, and never to let anything get in the way of what I wanted. Lying and stealing were what I did best (next to drinking), and I was secretly proud of my ability to manipulate and connive. The concept of a "common welfare" was totally alien to me, and to be expected to put the needs of others in front of my own was almost laughable. However, I was motivated by a desperation I can only describe as God-given, because without the certain knowledge that I was spiraling toward a very ugly death, I would never have been moved to accept those ideas. And I did accept them. I made a decision to accept this Tradition the same way I accepted the truth of the First Step, not because I fully understood all the implications and recognized their validity, but because I was desperate and I believed these were the only things that could save me.

I understood that the First Step was my lifeline to this program, and the First Tradition was the lifeline for the group. I understood that my recovery depended on AA unity. I even began to understand that it was just as important to me that others recovered because, for the first time in my life, I realized that I needed other people.

What I learned from the First Tradition changed the way I viewed the world and hence the way I interacted with others. Since this was the first time I looked at other people as important, and not as enemies,

I had to learn to listen to them. This was pretty difficult for someone like me. But as I got better at it, I was surprised to learn that there were an awful lot of smart, funny, nice people around. And people started to talk to me, and not just to say, "You keep coming, honey."

I learned to see the bigger picture, meaning AA beyond the groups I attended. I began to see the global power of AA, and I was able to trust AA to be my Higher Power. I have heard it said at meetings that when God sees the tiniest spark of willingness in your heart, he sends a thousand angels rushing to your side. Being able to accept AA as my Higher Power was that tiny spark of willingness, which opened my heart to hope. For me, this was the first gift of Tradition One. I had hope that this precious Fellowship would endure and that I could endure with it.

Another gift was the ability to work alongside others, whether it was to make coffee, reach out to a newcomer, or be a parent and a partner. (Truth be told, the parent and partner part was a long, slow process.) It didn't happen overnight, but I came to realize that I was having conversations with people during the break or while doing service. For the very first time in my life I knew the joy of being one among many, a worker among workers. For the very first time in my life I belonged somewhere, and it was in AA. I learned that putting AA ahead of myself didn't mean that I was "less than," it meant that I was part of. My greatest hope is that that never changes, and my greatest joy is that I know it never has to.

Kathleen D.
Shirley, New York

# If There Was No Group ...
January 1978
(From *Dear Grapevine*)

After a recent discussion meeting in which everyone shared the experience of using the AA principles in all their affairs, what came to my mind was the importance of Tradition One: "Our common welfare should come first; personal recovery depends upon A.A. unity."

Without the group, where would I be today? Would I be sober and happy? What if there had not been a group when my wife was searching for help for me, and for herself? What about the still-suffering alcoholic?

At first, I did not understand Tradition One, but today I can see how important it is to AA as a whole. Thank God for instilling this principle in our early members, and I hope I will always try to practice this Tradition.

R. T.
Massena, New York

# The Lifeboat
January 1994

I went to a meeting last week that taught me the importance of the First Tradition. Some time ago this group had decided to discuss one Step every month. They were on the Tenth Step that month, and I was looking forward to hearing everyone's experience, strength, and hope.

The chairperson started the meeting in the usual way, but then introduced his own topic. I asked him about the group's decision to discuss a Step every month. He said he knew about that, but he wanted to talk about something else. The rest of the people in the meeting didn't seem to care, and it wasn't my home group, so I didn't feel in a position to argue. The chairperson went on to talk about a relative who had checked into a treatment center. As I sat there pouting, I began to think about Bill W.'s analogy in *Twelve Steps and Twelve Traditions*. He said that the AA group is like a lifeboat. If everyone in the lifeboat is to survive, then everyone needs to stick together. I carried the analogy further. If a group follows the past experiences of our Fellowship (the Steps and the Traditions), it will be following in the wake of other boats. It will have a smoother ride.

The chairperson of that meeting was steering the boat. When he introduced his own topic, it was as if he took out a chainsaw and cut off his portion of the boat. He set the boat adrift. The next person talked about her concern for the way her daughter-in-law was raising the grandchildren. She took out another chainsaw and cut off her portion of the boat. The boat continued to break up as people brought up topics that had little to do with the common welfare of the group. As a group, they not only lost their ability to stay afloat, but they also lost their effectiveness in pulling in others who were still suffering.

After the meeting, I talked with a lady who had been sober and coming to meetings for nine months, but was about to check herself into an outpatient treatment program. Apparently she wasn't getting what she needed to stay sober in Alcoholics Anonymous.

My home group has a group conscience statement that's read at the beginning of every meeting. Part of it reads, "The format for our meeting tonight will be the discussion of a Step or Tradition of Alcoholics Anonymous. In keeping with AA's First Tradition, we respectfully ask that you confine your remarks to only the Step or Tradition being discussed. Other problems may be discussed after the meeting if you wish."

When I first started attending my home group, that statement really bothered me—because I wanted to talk about whatever moved me. Today I see that statement as saying, "Please check your chainsaw at the door."

Brian H.
Eau Claire, Wisconsin

## Response to May Grapevine
September 1992
(From *Dear Grapevine*)

I read with interest "Are We Locked In?" by E. L. of Council Bluffs. About those "noisy wet drunks" that come to our meetings, the First Tradition as written in *The Twelve Traditions Illustrated* spells out the answer. For E. L., I quote, "Our brother the noisy drunk affords the simplest illustration of this Tradition. If he insists on disrupting the meeting, we 'invite' him to leave and we bring him back when he's in better shape to hear the message. We are putting the 'common welfare (of the group)' first. But it is his welfare, too; if he's ever going to get sober, the group must go on functioning, ready for him."

During my 21 years in the Fellowship, I have been a part of groups that have asked "noisy wet drunks" to leave, but as the First Tradition suggests, in most every instance some of us in the group hung on to him (followed up) and, if still interested, we "brought him back" when he was in better shape to grasp the message.

D. A.
Lakeview, Arkansas

## Only Natural
January 2011

I was given the gift of sobriety a little over two years ago. I'm finding the love I once had for nature slowly returning. My passion for hiking, paddling, natural history and keeping a nature journal all faded away. I lost this passion during the last few years of my daily drinking and isolation, a sure sign of chronic alcoholism. It was my abiding love of the natural world that sustained me physically, emotionally and spiritually even at the bottom when I felt alienated from everything. My link to the natural world was my Higher Power hard at work while practicing anonymity.

Now, recovering from alcoholism, I've once again become an active volunteer for the agency that maintains my state's nature preserves. I venture out from time to time with a crew of biologists, botanists, herpetologists, entomologists and all kinds of other "ologists" to restore and maintain the rare and endangered species of plants, animals and their ecosystems. These good folks have taught me much about the intricate relationships these plants and animals have with one another as well as their unique habitats.

Not long ago I began reading about AA's Traditions and was struck by the similarities Tradition One has with the unity of the natural world I've learned about: how the individual parts make up the whole and the whole in turn makes life possible to continue on and pass on its endowments to the individuals yet to come. This perpetual dynamic seems to be at work in both the physical and spiritual worlds. Each unique individual plays an important role in the community, but on the flipside, each is only a little piece of the greater puzzle (which I still find puzzling but have come to believe in).

And so, at least to my reckoning, it seems that the dynamic process that unifies and perpetuates the unique habitats I help preserve is the same process at work in Alcoholics Anonymous: unity, service and recovery, each individual making a distinctive contribution to the whole.

This ecological paradox is beautifully expressed in the chapter about Tradition One in the "Twelve and Twelve": "Those who look closely soon have the key to this strange paradox. The AA member has to conform to the principles of recovery. His life actually depends upon obedience to spiritual principles. If he deviates too far, the penalty is sure and swift; he sickens and dies ... . Realization dawns that he is but a small part of the greater whole."

It appears to me that there is definitely something at work, something that offers individuals lavish liberty to be themselves (even to destruction) yet acts like a glue that bonds us together as a community or fellowship. The "Twelve and Twelve" defines this glue as "an irresistible strength of purpose and action." For each animal and plant, each alcoholic, there is a common bond: to stay alive, which for an alcoholic like me translates into staying sober with the help of AA and then passing on this legacy of unity and recovery. What is required from me is self-sacrifice to insure the common welfare. It's like a complete unbroken circle.

I am just now beginning to understand how I relate to the Fellowship of AA. What I've been taught working on nature preserves has shed some light on this "common welfare" mentioned in Tradition One. My individual liberty to act, think, talk or balk, as well as my sobriety, relies solely on my willingness and my complete surrender to the spiritual principles spelled out and conveniently numbered in the Twelve Steps and Twelve Traditions.

My sponsor told me early on that the AA program was a program of relationships. I didn't have a clue what he was talking about at the time. Now I think I'm finally catching on. It all began with striking up a relationship with a power greater than me. By Step Five I found myself stepping into a meaningful relationship with another human being. Now along comes the First Tradition, which spells out for me how to form a relationship with a community: that "crowd of anarchists," as the "Twelve and Twelve" so aptly defines us in the chapter on Tradition One.

I've witnessed this "strength of purpose and action" out on the nature preserves where I volunteer and am now witnessing it again here in the Fellowship of AA. Individual diversity is obviously not a weakness but a strength—a strength of purpose and action.

Just like the Twelve Steps, the Twelve Traditions are a pathway of spiritual progress. Being a chronic isolator at heart (I seem to have been born that way) I first went along with this unity/group deal because I was desperate and willing to try anything. As my sobriety lengthened from hours to days to months, I found out that this Tradition One ecology seemed to help keep me sober as it did others in my group. As time progressed I began to get a glimmer of the miraculous promises available to me by putting common welfare first. Instead of feeling diminished by being only a small part, I began to feel like I'd found a home, a place where I belonged after a lifetime of isolation and being fatally unique. Now I see that the spiritual principle of putting common welfare first is my proper relationship to the big picture—the whole deal—which in turn keeps me whole.

As I've witnessed out on the preserves and here in AA, when an individual flourishes and grows it greatly benefits the whole community that it is a small yet distinctive part of. And this is only possible if the community itself flourishes and grows. This same economy at work in nature is hard at work in the AA Fellowship. I'm not surprised. It seems to be how it works.

Ed C.
Bowling Green, Kentucky

# For the Good of the Group
January 2015

The other day someone at our home group had to be interrupted by one of the long-timers in the room. What could cause an interruption like this, you ask?

Our group conscience says that the needs of the group come before the individual ... in line with our First Tradition. The limited time we have available is for carrying the message, not for providing a forum for someone to carry out a rant about how their life is all messed up. We try to be as tolerant as we can, but sometimes the meeting needs to get back on track. Where did I learn this?

Some 25 years ago, when I was a newcomer, my life was a complete mess. I was in a treatment center and learned to express my feelings in the group. However, the folks in AA were not so sure that was the answer. A couple of times people in meetings with a lot more time than me explained that it was in the best interest of the group that the members practiced the principles. My sponsor explained that it was best for me to call him with my problems and not to use up the group's time to vent all my feelings. He told me that it was OK to share about a problem no more than three times at a meeting. And I needed to try and share what kind of a solution I was going to be applying to the problem. He wanted me to get away from wallowing in my problem with its accompanying self-pity. Sometimes he would just ask, "What Step are you on?"

It does take some courage to interrupt someone when they wander off track, but in the long run it's best for the group. In my case, it was best for me in the long run, too.

There are times, however, when interruptions in meetings are not necessarily for the good of AA. All too often I see a meeting interrupted with shouts of "Who are you?" when someone sharing inadvertently forgets to properly identify themselves. To me, this shows a lack of compassion and patience. Interruptions should be few and far between, such as when someone is disrupting the group. It's actually best to talk to someone after the meeting, so that they are not made to feel less than.

If you're ever in the Roseburg, Oregon area please stop in for a visit to my home group, the Brown Bag Group. It meets Monday through Friday at noon. You'll be made to feel welcome and will probably be asked to share. Newcomers are always welcome.

Ken T.
Tenmile, Oregon

# Unity Disrupted
January 1998

I will never forget the first time I really understood the meaning of Tradition One and how important our common welfare was to me personally. I was sitting in my home group meeting one morning a little after 7 A.M., not quite awake but aware that I was safe and among friends. These were the people who'd been there for me as I learned how to stay sober and live a life of love and service. Through the sharing of their own experience, I've learned the spiritual principles of the Steps and Traditions.

My home group is a large group that meets six days a week, has a lot of long-term sobriety and a very strong service structure. The monthly home group meetings (what we call business meetings) are often focused on what we can do to better carry the AA message to the newcomer. We celebrate birthdays by giving away AA literature and Grapevine. The minority is respected and encouraged to speak. As a result of this concerted effort to examine ourselves, our group continued to grow and prosper and attract newcomers.

That morning, a fellow (a new face) stood and began to hold forth, to preach really, about the Bible. Suddenly, I was no longer in a meeting of Alcoholics Anonymous but in a revival meeting. I was extremely uncomfortable and fearful. I wanted to say something, to interrupt him, but either I couldn't figure out a way to do it so as not to embarrass him or myself or I didn't have the courage. So I sat there looking at my feet, feeling miserable and hoping that any newcomers in the room would somehow know that this was not the message of AA.

After a few minutes, a member of the group interrupted the man—rather gruffly everyone later agreed—and told him that this was an AA meeting and that we really didn't want to hear about the Bible, and he asked him to sit down. The room heaved a silent and collective sigh of relief. Thank goodness someone had thought more of the group, thought more of our common welfare than of his own ego, and had the courage to speak up. There were a few seconds of awkward silence before the chairperson quickly called on someone else and the meeting got back on its normal footing.

Naturally, this incident was a topic of much discussion at the next home group meeting. It provided the basis for a lengthy discussion about Tradition One and how we could deal with disruptive people in the future. We all worried that telling someone that their sharing wasn't appropriate might jeopardize their sobriety. If embarrassed they might go out and drink. Others felt strongly that the welfare of the group as a whole was more important and that we had a responsibility to the newcomer to carry the message of AA. If our group failed in our primary purpose, newcomers would not be attracted to our meetings or worse yet, would not stay.

The result of this discussion was increased unity for the group. Everyone had their say and in the end we agreed that our common welfare as a group must come first. We would do our best to lovingly explain Tradition One to anyone who disrupted the group.

To participate in God's will through the group conscience process was a tremendous spiritual experience to me. I understood that in being a member of AA and of my home group, I was a part of something much greater than I was. For this I am truly grateful. The principle of putting AA's welfare above my own self-interest teaches me humility and self-sacrifice. These are principles that do not come naturally to a "me-first" alcoholic. But it's a tremendous way to live.

Anonymous
Maui, Hawaii

# It Only Takes Two

July 1997
(From *Dear Grapevine*)

I live in a remote town here in the Yukon Territories. Watson Lake boasts a population of about 1,700 residents. Our nearest city is Whitehorse, over 280 miles away, where two-thirds of the Yukon's population lives.

My home group has one meeting a week. Attendance is minimal. Sometimes I feel that because the same few people show up, my spirituality becomes deadened. Not often is there any new input into the group. Living in a small town doesn't readily lend itself to change, so it's easy to become complacent. In addition, our active involvement in AA as a whole is very restricted. Yet because I've decided to go to any length to stay sober, I'm always grateful for our Monday night meeting. The scarcity of our members and the lack of more meetings just makes me more aware of the true meaning of Tradition One: "Our common welfare should come first; personal recovery depends upon A.A. unity."

The Watson Lake group started with two dedicated members who faithfully attended each week for the first year and a half. These members set a fine example for me; they are living proof that it only takes two to have a meeting.

Living here in the Yukon, which is above the national average in alcohol consumption, I feel blessed to be a member of the Monday night meeting of Alcoholics Anonymous in Watson Lake. I want to thank each and every member for my sobriety.

Susan W.
Watson Lake, Yukon Territories

# Growing Pains
January 1998

The principle that "our common welfare comes first but that individual welfare follows close afterward," as expressed in the long form of Tradition One, was brought home to me in my early sobriety.

The Kihei Morning Serenity group (KMS) on Maui began in 1982 with a Friday morning meeting at 7 A.M. Originally held in an elementary school, KMS soon moved to a small public library in a group of community buildings consisting of an open hall, a cafeteria, an office and a tiny church across the common.

When KMS moved to the library, we met around one table in a corner, penned in by books. In Maui's young AA Fellowship, meetings of four or five people were very common and six or eight chairs usually sufficed, with a couple more available from the librarian's office if the meeting overflowed. In just a few months, however, an influx of newcomers and a few folks who had moved to Maui, brought KMS a bigger crowd. Some mornings it was as many as 20 people. Seeing a need, we expanded to Mondays as well. Eventually we had people sitting on the sills of the open windows and on the floor between the stacks on both days.

Soon, some long-timers joined with the new arrivals in calling for a change of meeting halls to accommodate the growing throng. A couple of enterprising members spoke with the pastor of the church across the common about the use of the hall behind the church. There was some concern on the congregation's part about overuse since meetings already met there on Monday, Tuesday, and Thursday evenings. However, they decided that renting their facilities to twelve-step groups was part of their mission, and they voted to allow us use of the hall.

When this information was brought before the group at the next home group meeting, a "loving debate" ensued. The group's conscience was finally put to a vote and everyone was in favor of moving—everyone, that is, except one lone holdout, an original member of the group. We asked him to voice his minority view, and while his reasons for staying put—he didn't think bigger was always better and he like the ambience of the library—didn't sway the group, he was very adamant about not moving. He said that if the group moved, he would no longer attend.

Well, this really threw the group into a dither. Some felt it was emotional blackmail, while others calmly asked, "How important is this move right now, anyway?" and still more reminded us, "We should never be in a hurry in AA." A second group conscience was taken and we voted to remain where we were until next month's home group meeting.

The next month's home group meeting was a repetition of the first. We all voted to move except the holdout who again said that if we moved, he would no longer attend. We still had the dilemma of people hanging from the windows and stacked up like cordwood in the aisles of the library, but the group once again voted in favor of the individual member and decided not to move for another month.

The third monthly home group meeting arrived and once again the move was the major topic. Once again the group voted to move the meeting. But—surprise!—the opposing member didn't raise his hand against the motion. The group wanted to know if this member would still attend the meeting when it moved. The member said he didn't know if he would attend but he could see there was a definite need to move and he no longer objected to the group conscience.

So, after three months, we felt we had sufficient unity to make the move and we did so promptly; the former opposing member did attend meetings in the new hall. Over the years, KMS has grown in size, and now 60 to a 100 members meet Monday through Saturday.

So, I learned firsthand that each AA member is a small part of a whole, and though every individual is important, he or she is not more important than the common welfare of the group.

D. E.
Wailuku, Hawaii

# TRADITION TWO

For our group purpose there is but one ultimate authority—
a loving God as He may express Himself in our group conscience.
Our leaders are but trusted servants; they do not govern.

———————◆———————

*The only power and authority to be found in AA stems from
the group conscience.*

During our drinking, many of us rebelled against anybody trying to tell us what to do. Yet we discover in AA that there are no bosses, the Fellowship is both a democracy and, in the words of Bill W., "a benign anarchy"—a perfect combination for those of us who found it difficult taking orders.

Once we sober up, and perhaps even attend a group business meeting or two, we begin to see that the group conscience can provide sure guidance without the weight of personalities and ego—that no AA can give another a directive and enforce obedience.

"When one person wants the group or meeting to do it his (or her) way only," writes Charlie W. in the story "Trusted Servants," "that is when Tradition Two comes in, because it is the group conscience that should prevail."

When facing difficult issues with the potential of tearing a group apart—to smoke or not to smoke, having open or closed meetings, being involved in the service structure or not—reliance on a loving God as expressed through the group conscience has often provided direction. Says the author of "When They Kept It Simple," "The principles of our program can bring me back from my self-centered opinions to a sincere consideration of what is best for AA, and therefore what is best for me."

# Who's In Charge?

February 2010

T radition Two helps us to sort out the always-tricky question: "Who is in charge?" After I came out of my alcoholic fog and looked around at the meetings, meeting rooms and members, I had a lot of questions. I needed to know who decided how meetings would be run, who the speakers would be and how the collection was spent. After attending meetings for a while, I noticed that there is quite a lot of menial labor required to keep the meetings running and the rooms open. Who does it and why? I'm sure I'm not the only one who came in with questions like these. But I was genuinely surprised as I learned the answers. AA is different from any other organization I've encountered. I'm as amazed today as I was then about how and why the Fellowship works.

The short answer is that "group conscience" runs AA at every level. Yes, we have volunteers for different jobs. However, they have no authority to decide anything; they merely have the responsibility to carry out the decisions of the group, or the "group conscience."

It would seem that an organizational structure like this would produce only chaos. At times, it does, but eventually everything gets sorted out—not always the way any particular member wants it to.

I saw this principle operating up front and personal in the first group that I joined. It was run by one individual who had been there for some years and made all the decisions about the group himself. Everyone else just wandered in and out. What happened was that when a serious problem faced the group, it fell apart. No one had enough interest to solve it. That group doesn't exist today.

When I attend business meetings today, the part of this Tradition that I try to remember is that it is a "loving" God expressed in our group conscience. Too often we are too human. I want to look smarter, more important or better informed; I want to see someone else put in his or her place; I want to squash what I think is a really stupid idea. Our business can and should be conducted in a loving way. I retain the gift of sobriety today.

I am just here to serve, and by doing so, I retain the gift of sobriety.

Nancy C.
Coconut Grove, Florida

# One Hot Texas Summer
February 2014

One of my favorite AA jokes is: What's the difference between a group conscience meeting and the Cub Scouts? The answer: The Cub Scouts have adult supervision! Another is: What's the biggest problem with a group business meeting? Answer: It's run by a bunch of drunks!

It was pointed out to me many years ago by an old-timer that the key word in Tradition Two is "may." "... there is but one ultimate authority—a loving God as He may express Himself in our group conscience."

Being taught early on that service to my home group is an obligation, not an option, I have been involved in business meetings almost from the beginning. But it hasn't always been an easy road for me to trudge.

What's always amazed me is that in most cases, we can be diametrically opposed on an issue, express those opinions during a business meeting, then hold hands and pray and exchange hugs afterward. That's been the case in almost every issue I've experienced, with one major exception: I had to watch my first home group die due to a break in this and other Traditions.

At that business meeting a well-respected old-timer found it necessary to attack another member. He felt she was abusing her use of the key to the meeting room by taking advantage of the air conditioning during the hot Texas summer. Rather than resolve the issue one-on-one, he chose to demand that something be done. The "discussion" turned quite ugly. What happened after that was painful.

Our group, which often had 30 to 40 members, split in two. Quite quickly, our group, which had a reputation in the area as one of the strongest around, imploded. People resigned offices and began attending other groups. Attendance went down and it began to become harder and harder to pay the bills. In a matter of months, the decision became very clear—it was time to close the doors. A group that had been so attractive to me when I first walked through the doors of AA, was gone. Locking the door for the last time was one of the hardest things I had to endure in my early sobriety.

Two other groups sprang from the ashes of that one, but neither could regain the lost momentum. Usually only five or six attended, maybe a dozen. After much struggling, they closed. The irony of the whole incident is that the two members of the original group had long made their amends to each other and had rebuilt their friendship.

In the years hence I've had three other home groups. At each, we've had our share of controversies: smoking or non-smoking, open or closed meetings, literature-based or open discussion, involvement in the service structure or non-involvement, the usual distractions. Through it all, our members for the most part have experienced the unity we so desperately need through the Traditions.

In the appendices of the Big Book, the introduction to the AA Tradition reads: "... no society of men and women ever had a more urgent need for continuous effectiveness and permanent unity. We alcoholics see that we must work together and hang together, else most of us will finally die alone."

During any controversy at a group conscience meeting, I always try to keep in mind what that old-timer told me so long ago, that the key word in Tradition Two is "may." But whether God expresses himself or the decision is made because of a handful of "bleeding deacons," my home group is still my family.

My prayer is that I never again have to experience what I went through in my first home group. But if I do, I hope we can resolve those differences with the help of God and continue to hang together. We must, because the option our co-founder pointed out is to die alone, and by incorporating the program in our daily lives, that should not have to be an option for any of us.

Anonymous

---

# Try It Standing Up
July 2000

I'm very protective of my home group for the same reason that most alcoholics are: if the group doesn't survive, neither will I. A couple of months ago at a business meeting, my home group had a heated discussion over whether or not to say the Lord's Prayer at the end of our group's meetings. Saying it certainly seems to contradict AA's claim to have no affiliations with any sect or denomination. Furthermore, as a skittish newcomer, I remember being very uncomfortable sitting in a church basement saying a prayer that's a prominent part of Christian liturgy.

But my sponsor said, "Get over it." And I have to admit, it has never hurt me to say a prayer, especially one conceived by a loving teacher, teaching me to praise God's name, to wish for God's will to be done, and to remind myself I will be forgiven only to the degree that I forgive others.

The Lord's Prayer certainly feels paternalistic. (So, does that mean we should be saying the Hail Mary instead?) The Serenity Prayer may feel less sectarian, but it stems from religion, too. So in that case, rather than wishing to shut the door on our past, maybe we should acknowledge AA's debt to the Oxford Movement, Reverend Shoemaker, Father Dowling, and Sister Ignatia, just to name a few.

Have I managed to offend you yet? To get your juices going? Because that's what happened at our business meeting. We all got churned up and disagreeable. And afterward, there was a hangover, a lingering air of resentment. Now when we form a circle and join hands at the end of our regular meeting, we all feel the tension. A moment that used to exemplify our unity now underscores our differences.

The idea that issues and resentments generated in a business meeting are spilling over into the "real" meeting troubles me. I suppose without business meetings, resentments might smolder anyway, but I think we fanned the fire. I got the feeling that things were just going too smoothly for us drama-loving alcoholics, so we latched onto something controversial to add a little excitement to the proceedings.

To the extent that we were just "stirring the pot," we were following a longstanding tradition in AA. But not the Traditions of Alcoholics Anonymous. One Tradition calls for us to "practice a genuine humility" and to silence "the clamor of desires and ambitions whenever these could damage the group." For me, that clamor is the need to comment on everything, to throw in my two cents so you'll know just how smart I am. It's the urge to jump in and mix it up as if a business meeting were a barroom brawl. I need to practice some restraint, to emulate the example of the elder statesman in Tradition Two who "is willing to sit quietly on the sidelines patiently awaiting developments."

My friend G. had an interesting suggestion: why not hold our business meetings standing up? I know I'd pontificate less if I had to stand more. How often have I told myself, If I have to sit through this meeting, then I should at least get to air my point of view, even if it's already been expressed by several others. Maybe our feet are better judges of when we've said enough than our minds.

And if business meetings were shorter and to the point, maybe more people would get involved. Since our group conscience is how the loving God expresses himself to us, the more conscience, the more God, right? Let the primary purpose of a business meeting be to make sure the rent is paid, the key positions are filled, and there's enough literature and sponsorship available to help the newcomer. Keep it simple. Tradition Nine says, "Alcoholics Anonymous needs the least possible organization." Save the controversy for a letter to Grapevine.

Our "meeting in print" has shown for over 50 years that it can handle controversy. It even thrives on it.

Of course, I should have a bit more faith in my group's ability to weather contentious business meetings. What doesn't kill us makes us stronger. In which case, I have just made much ado about nothing. I probably should have written this standing up.

J. W.
Maplewood, New Jersey

# Trusted Servants
March 1995
(From *Dear Grapevine*)

Without sounding like a bleeding deacon myself, I think many people in AA would benefit from reading and examining Tradition Two. On examining this Tradition, I thought of people in AA who try to push their dogma on the rest of us and on our groups and meetings. When one person wants the group or meeting to do it his (or her) way only, that is when Tradition Two comes in, because it is the group conscience that should prevail at our business meetings and meetings in general.

Unfortunately for us, some people in AA think God put them on earth to tell the rest of us what they think we ought to do with our lives, whether we like it or not. But we don't have to do anything we don't want to do. To me, that is the beauty of Tradition Two, because it protects us from people like that! I think the Traditions have kept AA together for the last 50 plus years, and they will keep us together for the long run.

So, remember the Second Tradition when someone is trying to enlighten you against your wishes. You don't have to do it and neither does the group.

Charlie W.
Tucson, Arizona

# Our Way, Not My Way

February 2008

When I was drinking, I didn't want anyone telling me what to do, mostly because I was afraid they'd tell me to stop drinking. Getting sober has required letting someone tell me what to do, not as a demand, but as a life-or-death suggestion (like taking a parachute along when you jump from an airplane). When first humbled by my alcoholism, I found it easy to follow instructions. As a result, I developed a lot of habits that are good for maintaining my sobriety, such as going to meetings, reading the literature, doing service work, etc. But as time marched on, I found some new suggestions harder to swallow. I also found myself with a bit of what I call sober pride, which is the belief that I know about AA and staying sober since I have such-and-such time away from my last drink. It's logical. If I have time, I must be doing something right. If I'm doing something right, then I should know what that is. Maybe I know what's best for me now. Maybe I even know what's best for you.

My home group has a nice way of taking its inventory on a regular basis. Every month, we get together and ask ourselves two simple questions: "Are we really serving the newcomers?" And, "Are we really following the Traditions?" This has occasionally led to some self-congratulations on how well we have been doing. At other times, it has led to divisive discussions that last through several months of group conscience meetings. One month, I brought up an observation about the group's diversity. It seemed that fewer and fewer women were staying in our group. I appreciate the greatest variety of experience, including the female point of view, on staying sober and living life one day at a time. What I didn't expect was that the conclusion drawn by the group as to why this was happening and what to do about it would feel like a major slap in my face.

The group concluded that women weren't staying in our meeting because of the foul language bandied about among the men. This seemed ironic to me, since one of our worst offenders had, in fact, been a woman. Nevertheless, the group decided to add to our meeting's opening statement a request that people please use polite language (whatever that meant).

I was outraged. To me, this smacked of censorship. I was also afraid that if we sanitized the meeting too much, newcomers might feel out of place and might not want to come back. I was mostly livid because it meant that I was going to have to change my behavior, when what I really wanted to change was all those people who voted for the proposal.

I had a choice to make. Either I could follow their edict or rebel and do things my way. I saw my ignoring the will of the group conscience as a form of counter vote. A minority opinion, if you will. This wasn't without precedent in our group history. One time we had asked people to stop speaking more than once during a given meeting so that all would have the chance to share.

Evidently, some people didn't agree and continued to share two, three, even four times in a single meeting, but there was nothing the group could do. We couldn't make anyone conform (nor did we as a group want to—though I did). But when pondering the rebellion strategy, I couldn't bring myself to do it. I was afraid to disregard the group's decision. Not because I was afraid of being ostracized, but because I thought about the humility I needed when I first got sober and how much that had served me in creating the wonderful sober life I have today. I wasn't sure if my defiance would be an honest, concerned part of me seeking to correct a "wrong," or my alcoholic denial and rationalization system back up in full swing trying to isolate me from the group through resentment and pride.

So I decided to give group will a try. Through gritted teeth, I began to censor my own speech in the discussions. Gone were the "f-bombs" and taking the name of some members' Higher Power in vain.

I searched for new ways to express myself, my resentments, and my fears. The meeting began to sound a lot less like a bar and more like some sort of civic league. I was afraid we might be becoming too Pollyannish and the newcomer might feel like a fish out of water.

Slowly, I began to notice another change, not in the group, but in me. Eventually, I found it easier to avoid street talk. I guess it wasn't as important as I once thought. But the biggest change came from being forced to talk about my anger and fears in new ways. Instead of just cursing, I had to explain how I felt and why.

This growing self-awareness led me to more fully understand the nature of my resentments and deep-rooted fears and how they form in my mind. It helped me get to the "stuff" behind the defects. I began to realize that the things I was angry at were really diversions from a deeper pain that often troubled me, and by getting into that, as opposed to covering it all up with violent language, I was able to face my "causes and conditions" (Big Book, page 64) and work through them. All of a sudden, I was once again experiencing that feeling I had as a newcomer of having my heart opened up and the contents lovingly exposed to the light.

I remembered when I was new and listened to other people share the truth of what they had experienced as active alcoholics. It had touched me deeply. It had given a voice to a pain that had been hammered down into my darkest places by my drunkenness. A place inside me opened up and received the grandest welcome home ever.

I remembered my first stumbling words when I tried to tell other human beings how I really felt on the inside. I kept looking at their faces to see if they were comprehending what it was I was saying. I was cracking my shell open to tell them what lay inside (they didn't always understand, but they always smiled and listened to it all, anyway).

Loneliness has vanished. But this time, it's not because I have people around me again, but because I have started to let them in, and I am letting them in through the language of the heart and not of the street. But I would have never known this if it weren't for an expression of love that came through the group conscience.

Dan B.
Rochester, New York

# Feed Them and They Will Come
February 2013

In my first year of being a GSR, my home group called a group conscience. The church we met in had recently made our meeting go non-smoking, which at that time cut our attendance by about a third. Then some good old-fashioned disagreements between members caused a split (all healthy of course), and suddenly we were down to six core members. The topic of our group conscience was whether or not we could keep our doors open. My sponsor said that the doors were open when he got here, and that as long as we simply stayed "in the books," we would survive. We unanimously agreed.

We younger members were big on attendance and growth. One young lady suggested that we change our weekly speaker meeting to an "eat and speak." Enthusiasm climbed as we talked of how great the idea seemed. Feed them, and they will come! All we needed to do was make sure that each of us brought an oversize dish to make sure we had enough to feed the crowds that would come. Oh, how we would grow.

My sponsor, the voice of wisdom on the previous matter, quietly sat back and listened as we bantered about the proposed opportunity for growth. Finally he spoke: "We've done this a couple of times before, and it's always started out good, but eventually it ends up with just a few of the same people doing all of the work and leads to problems and resentments. If we just stay in the books, I'm sure the growth will come and we'll be fine." The vote went four to two in favor of the eating meeting. We set a date, and I figured we could carry the meeting without his help.

The day came, and just as we got started, my sponsor walked in and asked me to help him carry in an ice chest full of sodas, plus a large casserole and a peach cobbler. He showed up early and stayed late at every eating meeting we had. We lasted three or four months before the workload took its toll. He never once said "I told you so."

When I asked him how come he went ahead and participated when he obviously didn't agree, he simply said, "God speaks through the group conscience, and he knows better than me what's best for us all."

Hopefully, his example will always remind me to respect the group's conscience—that his will, not necessarily mine, be done.

Harold C.
Nicoma Park, Oklahoma

# When They Kept It Simple
February 2006

I belonged to an Eleventh Step group in a small village out in the country during my first year of sobriety. We met on Sunday mornings in the village grange, and the meeting was quite popular. We regularly drew about 60 people who came for our 10-minute meditation, followed by a speaker/discussion meeting.

The village was small and parking was tight, especially during the summer when tourists came to visit the surrounding countryside. Occasionally, the town's police officer would come in during the meeting to say we had to move such-and-such car away from a driveway, or that we were blocking some important access. The group realized that we had outgrown our space and discussions began on finding a larger space with better parking accommodations. This may sound like a simple proposition, but it became a volatile issue.

Many people loved the grange, and felt threatened by the prospect of moving. The meeting had been there for many years and some of us believed the spirituality of the meeting had infused the cinder block walls with a special feeling.

Our business meetings became difficult and more emotional as we discussed whether or not we should move. People interrupted one another to get their point across, and some ill will developed. I started to dread business meetings because I felt confused. The meeting itself could be so spiritual, nurturing and loving, but the business meeting was governed more by insecurity, fear and hurt feelings.

Then a member of the group with more than 10 years of sobriety suggested that we begin our business meetings by reading the Second Tradition: "For our group purpose there is but one ultimate authority—a loving God as He may express Himself in our group conscience. Our leaders are but trusted servants; they do not govern."

The group chairperson followed the Second Tradition reading with a short statement that said, "We are holding this group conscience to discover our Higher Power's will about moving the meeting. We ask each member who participates in these discussions to do their best to leave their personal opinions out of their comments, to respect the comments of others, and to sincerely try to consider what's best for our group." This statement brought calm to our business meetings and returned civility and respect to our group conscience process.

Ultimately, the group conscience decided that we move the meeting to the local fire station where there was more parking and where our presence was less of a burden to the village. We got used to sitting among the fire trucks and now those walls, too, have been infused with the spirituality of our meditations, prayers and discussions. I learned a valuable personal lesson during this process. The principles of our program can bring me back from my self-centered opinions to a sincere consideration of what is best for AA, and therefore what is best for me.

C. M.
Pittsfield, Massachusetts

# TRADITION THREE

The only requirement for A.A. membership is a desire
to stop drinking.

———————— ◆ ————————

*We're members of AA when we say we are—there is no
other qualification.*

"My name is Mickey and I'm an alcoholic," writes one AA in this
chapter's story, "Where I Belong." "When I make this simple
statement in an AA meeting, I seldom think about what a profound truth it expresses. I'm saying I belong, and I'm choosing to be a
part of this Fellowship ... No one had to approve my application—in
fact there was no application."

It wasn't always this way, however. Early on, many AA groups had
stringent rules and regulations regarding membership. Asked to list
these requirements and send them to "AA Headquarters," Bill W. re-
marked, "If all of these edicts had been in force everywhere at once,
it would have been practically impossible for any alcoholic to have
joined AA."

Recognizing how restrictive such rules and regulations could be, it
was determined to throw the doors of AA wide open. Since then, many
have been the grateful beneficiaries of this Tradition, much like Jack
B., the author of "Three Strikes, You're In!" Young, gay and agnostic,
he entered AA "with feelings of worthlessness, fear of rejection and
shame." He found, however, that the Fellowship made him feel like he
belonged—for the first time in his life. "I owe a debt of gratitude to those
who supported me and accepted me as I am," he writes. "As a result, I'm
at peace with myself and life is good."

# Where I Belong
March 1998

For as far back as I can remember, I never believed I belonged anyplace. When I was growing up I didn't feel I belonged in my family, in the little town that I lived in, in the church I attended, or in the schools where I was educated. I was never chosen for a team or for membership in any group.

My name is Mickey and I'm an alcoholic. When I make this simple statement in an AA meeting, I seldom think about what a profound truth it expresses. I'm saying I belong, and I'm choosing to be a part of this Fellowship.

Thanks to Tradition Three, I'm the only person in that AA meeting who can make that choice. Only I can know if, in my innermost self, I have a desire to stop drinking. And because this desire is the only requirement for membership in AA, I'm the only person who can say whether I meet that membership criterion.

When I first became aware of Tradition Three, I realized it made it possible for me to stay in AA. No one had to approve my application—in fact there was no application. It didn't matter whether others believed I was an alcoholic or had a desire to stop drinking. They may have had an opinion, but only I had that inner knowledge.

It was unimportant if I had other problems or other abilities—these things might be significant to me, but they had no bearing on my membership in Alcoholics Anonymous. And the things which might affect my ability to belong to other organizations—age, sex, race, religion, marital status, profession, etc.—had no value here. In fact I didn't even need to reveal these things to be accepted in AA.

It was only much later that I began to glimpse the reverse side of this coin—that being accepted with no conditions other than a desire to stop drinking imposed upon me the responsibility of accepting others equally. I saw that having no requirements placed upon us gave each of us the freedom to become what our Higher Power intended, without artificial restrictions.

In developing the ability to freely accept other alcoholics, I've discovered that the similarities that bind us and make us a part of this Fellowship mean far more than all the superficial differences that always kept me from that feeling of belonging. Today I thank my Higher Power that I finally know where I belong. I belong in Alcoholics Anonymous.

Mickey H.
Springville, Utah

# Religious Indifference
March 2011

Over my years in AA I have had the opportunity to attend jail and prison meetings in three different states. When I moved home to North Carolina in 2004 I was happy to be able to attend corrections meetings in this state as well.

There is a men's minimum-security prison here in my hometown and I became one of the outside sponsors for its weekly AA meeting. Because it is a minimum-security facility, many men are serving short sentences or have achieved minimum-security status after serving time in a higher-security prison. Some are nearing their release dates, so the turnover of the men attending the AA meetings is fairly high. A few fortunate inmates at this facility are permitted to attend outside meetings with an AA sponsor. Because of the turnover, I usually take three or four different men to the outside meetings each year.

Last Friday night was the first time I took Grant F. to an outside meeting. About the only things I knew about Grant were that he attended the prison AA meeting regularly, one of the inmates I sponsor recommended him, he sounded like he had been sober for a while and he was currently serving as an officer of his group. When I picked up Grant at the prison I noticed that he was wearing a kufi. (Kufis are traditional skull caps worn by Muslim men.) As we pulled up to our AA building I noticed that Pam B., our "Cookie Lady," was carrying in some freshly baked cookies for our meeting. I told Grant that he was in for a treat and to please enjoy her cookies as we introduced him to everyone at the meeting.

Our Friday night meeting is a Big Book study meeting and we were on the Eleventh Step, starting on the bottom of page 85. Our practice is to read a few paragraphs and then comment on what was read. We had a small number of people at our meeting and there was plenty of time for everyone who wished to share. Most of us commented about our religious upbringings and how we had learned to pray and to rely on prayer. Almost everyone in the room besides Grant had identified himself or herself as a Catholic or a Protestant as they shared about their experience with prayer. Grant said that he had had some concerns about coming to our meeting because he is a Muslim and was not sure how he would be received. He said that prayer was a big part of his religion and that he prays every day.

I told Grant I was glad that he was there. The doors to AA are very wide. Our Third Tradition states, "The only requirement for A.A. membership is a desire to stop drinking." AA has no litmus test for deciding whether or not you can join AA other than the desire to stop drinking. We do not ask your politics, your profession, your marital status, your favorite sports teams, your religion or even if you have one. I said that I had been raised as a Southern Baptist and they do not believe in drinking alcohol. Muslims do not believe in drinking alcohol either, yet there we both were, in an AA meeting on a Friday night in Sanford, North Carolina. When I dropped Grant off at the prison after the meeting, I asked him if he wanted to go again the next week. He wanted to know if there would be more cookies.

There is no small print in the Third Tradition. There is no application to fill out, no initiation fee, no screening committee and no rulebook. AA is working for so many of the diverse people in the meetings I attend.

John K.

Sanford, North Carolina

# Are We Locked In?
May 1992

I went to a meeting this last Saturday night. The usual stuff was happening. You know, hot coffee, and people laughing and sharing.

We started the meeting with the Preamble, a reading and a topic. Then a wet drunk came in. He staggered in, found a chair and pronounced he was an alcoholic. You could tell that the man lived on the streets. I thought, Oh this is wonderful. I had a new sponsee there— first meeting since treatment. She was nervous and so were the other newcomers. I said, "It's OK. We need him."

To my surprise, the woman chairing the meeting was angry, along with three other people, all four with several years of sobriety. They told the man if he couldn't be quiet he'd have to leave. They were louder than he was. In a short time the woman and one of the men got up and escorted the alcoholic out the door. One of them told him to shut up. In a few minutes he came back in, said he'd be quiet, and sat back down. But being drunk, he couldn't be good enough. Again, they began to escort him to the door.

I was angry and said he had a right to be there. The Third Tradition ensures him a place. But they wouldn't hear me. This time they locked him out.

I was shocked, appalled and angry. I was always told that the only requirement is a desire to stop drinking, that "any alcoholic is a member if he says he is." I didn't realize we could say "No, not you. You're dirty, drunk and noisy!"

One gentleman told me that if a drunk is disruptive then we have a right to kick him out. I thought, How intolerant. I wonder how many times we as drunks were disruptive in bars, in restaurants, on the streets. Weren't we disruptive when we were out there? How many times I had come home drunk, to disrupt my family, neighbors and friends! I wonder where I'd be if, when I came to my first meeting, I had been locked out, my last hope locked away from me. It is scary that one alcoholic could lock another out.

The "Twelve and Twelve" mentions "early intolerance based on fear." I saw a lot of fear that evening. Some didn't want to see the dirty drunk; I guess he reminded them from where they came. Our pride gets hurt once we're all cleaned up. The Fifth Tradition states that "Each group has but one primary purpose—to carry its message to the alcoholic who still suffers." I wonder if they felt he wasn't suffering enough.

There were four people who said they had wanted to drink that day. After our friend was there none of them had the desire to drink. There were five newcomers that night. All of them were confused. Why do we say that all alcoholics are welcome and then throw one out and lock the door?

I am worried about what message we carry to the newcomers. Where are our principles? Where is our compassion, our tolerance? And where is our future going to be if we lock the door on the new-comers?

How can we survive, grow and carry out our primary purpose without the drunks? Will the hand of Alcoholics Anonymous be there if you or I get drunk? How would Bill W. or Dr. Bob feel about locking out a drunk?

Well, I need to say the Serenity Prayer!

E. L.
Council Bluffs, Iowa

# Three Strikes, You're In!
March 2014

When I came to AA at age 21 I had to overcome not one, not two, but three obstacles that made getting sober more challenging than it needed to be. The first hurdle was that I was too young. There were nothing but older folks in my first few meetings, leaving me feeling alone and very different. The average age in the room was more than double mine.

Second was that I was gay. I knew I had to be the only gay person in AA for sure. Everyone was talking about his or her spouse, while I hadn't even had a real adult relationship yet.

Finally, I considered myself to be either an agnostic or an atheist. As a result of my religious upbringing, I entered AA with feelings of worthlessness, fear of rejection and shame. Meetings often closed with the Lord's Prayer, and were filled with numerous references to God. I thought there was no way this Fellowship was going to be right for me.

But I was desperate and had nowhere else to turn. In one of those early meetings someone said, "The only requirement for membership is a desire to stop drinking." That, I surely had. My drinking was daily and around the clock. And even though I was "too young," I was consuming mass quantities of alcohol and having blackouts all the time. So even though I felt terribly unique, I needed what AA had to offer to stop drinking. So I stayed.

It's been 32 years since those early days, and it's almost embarrassing for me to admit that only in the past year have I been completely open about my identity in mainstream meetings. I feel a growing obligation to share about the hurdles that held me back in those early days of my recovery. Now I can share this for those who may struggle similarly—and for myself. My openness is the best indication of my own self-acceptance.

So dare to be as authentic as you can. Sameness is boring. I am grateful my terminal uniqueness didn't chase me away from AA. Today I celebrate the differences that made the beginning of my recovery difficult. The Fellowship made me feel like I belonged for the first time in my life. I owe a debt of gratitude to those who supported and accepted me as I am. As a result, I'm at peace with myself and life is good. Thanks to the Third Tradition.

Jack B.
Oakland, New Jersey

# Whose Rules?
October 2001
(From *Dear Grapevine*)

I read with dismay the letter "Stand Fast" in the June 2001 issue. The Third Tradition states: "The only requirement for A.A. membership is a desire to stop drinking." It says nothing about having to present ourselves in any particular fashion, especially not in a manner conducive to recovery. This is just a rule the writer's sponsor made up for himself (or got from someone else). Thank God that this isn't a fact for us all. I would never have made it 13 years if someone had told me I had to behave, or dress, a certain way. My sponsor told me to go to meetings and not drink in-between, work the Steps, pray daily, and call her if I felt like drinking. Just that was a pretty tall order for me. More power to Anonymous for staying sober with someone laying non-AA "rules" on him.

By the way, people I stay sober with sometimes go to meetings in drag, and many have been sober far longer than I. Gay people can, and do, stay sober.

Mike H.
Seattle, Washington

# Time Will Tell
March 2013

There was a time in my early recovery when everything was perfect—no resentments, no hostility, no personality was too much for me. I was just happy to be sober. The Living Sober Group in the Great Utah Valley met every day at noon and a few nights a week. It was an oasis to my dreary eyes. Things couldn't have started to get better fast enough. But then the tough question was asked: Am I an alcoholic?

Some people will tell you that they knew they were alcoholic long before they came into the program. Not me; I thought I struggled with drug addiction mainly. At 16 my drinking career slowed way down when drugs took over my life, so much so that I couldn't waste my time with just alcohol. Life was spiraling out of control; consequences became too much. I had to find relief somewhere.

AA is where I found it. So I figured I would just claim I was alcoholic even though I wasn't convinced. All I knew was that it is better to be sober than to be loaded, and if I had to say I was an alien from Pluto I would have said it. You people were helping me in a way no one ever had.

There were some old-timers who would say, "Alcoholics Anonymous is for alcoholics only." My heart would sink to my feet when I heard that. Once again I started to feel like an intruder, my membership status a charade. What happens when they find me out? Am I welcome?

Then one day I finally came to the conclusion that I was in fact an alcoholic. I have a good friend who used to say "I caught alcoholism through my ears." That was true for me too. I listened and heard my story told by people who said they were alcoholics. They looked just like me, they talked just like me, and the way they felt was the way I felt too.

Looking back at my past, I saw what the Big Book calls countless vain attempts to prove I was a normal drinker. Drugging was just another vain attempt for me.

In all fairness, not all the old-timers were bent on challenging my alcoholism. Most were loving, kind and tolerant through my "alcoholic/addict" phase, giving me the time I needed to find out for myself what I am—a grateful alcoholic.

I'm now approaching four years in AA, and I often pause and ask myself: Am I giving that confused newcomer a chance to figure it out? Am I so caught up in making sure that the Third Tradition is upheld that I'm trampling the others? What right do I have to decide for another whether they're alcoholic or not? Is it not their call only? Do I remember my responsibility?

Thank you for giving me a chance to figure it out.

Thank you for telling me to keep coming back.

Thank you for loving me when I didn't have the capacity to love myself.

Thank you for showing me how to be responsible, when all I knew how to do was create chaos and pain.

And I thank you for being an alcoholic—just like me.

Anonymous

# You Just Never Know
May 1991

My home group's meetings are regularly disrupted by a young man who suffers from what seems to be an emotional or mental disorder of some kind. He is extremely restless, and wanders around during the meeting, talking to himself. He laughs wildly at what I deem inappropriate times. He flirts with the women by raising his eyebrows up and down at them, all the while flashing a broad smile with ill-preserved teeth. His clothing is soiled, his hair often a matted mess. He attends and shares regularly and, although what he shares seems to be for the most part unintelligible, disjointed "AA speak," he does seem to be a little more grounded in reality than he was at first.

There was talk at a business meeting of permanently removing him from our meetings. But, by the grace of God, the Third Tradition kicked in and everyone was reminded that this young man should be as welcome at our meetings as any others who think they have a problem with alcohol.

I've always regarded him as little more than a disruptive presence, someone to be tolerated. Occasionally, during my more spiritual moments, I've been able to see my reaction to him as an opportunity for growth. I've often felt grateful that I was never that bad. Well, there's never a dull moment in the spiritual life, and more was soon revealed when an AA friend called the other day to tell me the following incident:

"We had a female newcomer at the meeting this morning. It was her first AA meeting. The meeting began and the young man started up with his usual pestering. First he brought the woman coffee from the kitchen. Then he made another trip to the kitchen to get cream and sugar. He returned and sat down next to her, giggling and babbling like he always does. He introduced himself and asked what her name was.

"He shuffled and clunked around the room some more with his coffee. At the literature rack he picked out a few pamphlets and took them over to the woman. She looked scared, but she put the bundle on her lap. Then he got up again, and headed for the bulletin board. He stood there for a while, reading. He went to the kitchen again for more coffee. He wandered outside, then he wandered back in. He made another stop in the kitchen. We heard him laughing hysterically. Inwardly I noted, typical. He's the only one who ever seems to be able to hear the punchlines of these cosmic jokes. He sat down again. His hand went up, and he identified himself as an alcoholic."

Identified himself as an alcoholic. You are a member when you say so, right? Well, he said so. Hmmm.

Yes, carrying on a conversation while someone else is sharing is rude. But my friend's story was beginning to make me think. I could try to adjust my perceptions and see that the young man was, in his own inimitable manner, extending a welcoming hand to the newcomer. Should it matter that I find it difficult, if not impossible, to understand anything he's ever said? Or that I seriously doubt that he's really an alcoholic, or that he's ever read the Big Book, or worked any Steps? Isn't he just plain crazy?

The Big Book talks a lot about insanity. Our insanity. Yours and mine. It says we need to be restored to sanity. Is it possible that I am just as crazy as this guy, but my type of insanity is more socially acceptable? And by the way, since when did a bunch of alcoholics ever really know anything about the proper rules of social conduct in the first place? But darn it, I've been really exasperated with this guy. I find his behavior distracting; I'm suspicious of his motives. I sometimes think he is a threat, albeit a small one, to what is perceived as being the AA way, as I understand it. He just won't play by "my" rules.

But what if I consider the possibility that I am here for the same reasons he is? Couldn't my own alcoholism be just another form of the same grave emotional and mental disorder I have so neatly diagnosed in him? Why do I assume that his disorder is any worse, or causes any more unmanageability, than my own? Aren't I, also, one of "those who suffer"? Haven't I already admitted that I need to be restored to sanity? Do I think I have a monopoly on the correct way to work the program? Since when am I in charge of enforcing specific requirements for membership? Just who do I think I am, anyway?

Back to my friend's story:

"We were beginning to squirm watching him scare off another newcomer again, so after the meeting a few of us went over to the woman. 'Please,' one of us said, 'Don't let him scare you off. We've all had to put up with him. He's really harmless.'

"The woman said, 'Oh! I picked him up hitchhiking. He brought me to this meeting.' If there was a cosmic joke, the joke was on me. I could only suppose that God, in his infinite wisdom—and with style to spare—had chosen to reveal a glimpse of the workings of his will.

"Once again, I got to see how little I really know, what a tiny piece of God's reality I am able to perceive at any given moment—and just how narrow my perceptions and judgments often are. How utterly wrong.

"Today I'm grateful that a power greater than myself is always hard at work behind the scenes, performing miracles with no help whatsoever from me. My job is simply to stay out of his way and to remember that I'm in trouble when I think I know something."

As I listened to my friend finish telling the story, I was overwhelmed with a feeling of humility, and I got another chance to sit back and appreciate the awesome miracle of God and the AA program at work.

Anonymous

# Ready to Bolt
March 2015

As a child, I was curious about religion. Since my dad was an atheist he didn't want his children attending church. While he was adamant about his feelings, he did not ban us from going to services. However, my dad demanded equal time, so when I crept back home from Sunday services, he would ask me about the nature of the sermon I had just heard in church. Then he'd lecture me against the religion I was interested in. At that phase of my life, I considered my dad's lectures a bunch of bull. Later, while attending theology classes in college, I learned that my barely educated father was more learned than I thought. As far as I was concerned, my study of religion was over. I decided I too was an atheist.

As an atheist, I had reservations about joining AA. From the bits and pieces of information I had, I thought that AA was a religious program. Even though I wanted to be sober, I felt that I could not sacrifice my beliefs for the sake of sobriety. It seemed too big of an emotional expense, so I decided I had to do it alone.

Since I was somewhat successful at not drinking, I kept plugging away at sobriety—relapse after relapse. Sometimes I'd stay sober for a year or two and then I'd slip and drink for a while, until a drunken incident convinced me that I was out of control. Once more, I would white-knuckle it until I lost my grip on sanity. I'd rationalize that my behavior was too austere; I had to chill out. I'd make plans to drink like a normal person. It would work for a while; then my resolve would weaken and I'd go out again on a binge. Usually an incident would bring me back to reality.

One night, while driving home with one eye closed, I was wondering when this farce would end. A red light from a police car answered that question. This was my first DUI. Once again I had an incentive to quit drinking. As I aimed my pickup to the roadside, I told myself I'd never have another drink. I didn't know how I would accomplish the assignment, but I knew I would go to any length to do it.

The next morning, instead of trying to keep my arrest a secret, I telephoned my ex-wife, my children and my sisters. Since they live in different communities, it was unlikely they'd have learned of my arrest. I felt that the humiliation of being truthful would reinforce my commitment to sobriety. And since I figured I'd be mandated to attend AA, I thought I should start going to meetings before I was ordered to.

As I entered the room for my first AA meeting, I was scared. I knew that this was a fork in the road. More than likely, I thought, this decision would change my life forever. Little did I know how much. I took the seat nearest to the door. I was ready to exit at the first mention of God. It didn't take long. As someone read the Preamble and the Traditions, God was mentioned over and over again. I was on the verge of bolting when I noticed the Third Tradition on the wall. I certainly had the desire to quit drinking; that meant that I had a right to stay there. So I did.

At first, I was so busy reacting to the word God that I didn't hear all the words being said. After a while, I learned that when some of the people said the word God they weren't referring to a divine entity. They were referring to a "Group of Drunks," the "Great Outdoors" or the "Gift of Desperation." That was when I started to calm down. From that moment on, I started to hear and appreciate the messages. I realized that there is a place in this program for a person with my beliefs. I just had to stop fighting and accept everything for its own value. I had to respect other people's choices. And I had a choice of making whatever was said part of my program or not. Since I identified with most drunkalogs, it wasn't hard for me to choose a group of drunks as my Higher Power. As I started to understand, I realized that my fellow drunks had the answer to my dilemma of how to stay sober. They reinforced my commitment and advised me of alternative behaviors. Like my successful predecessors, I just had to work the Steps, get a sponsor and do service.

Yes, it wasn't always so simple, but each day I learned more and made some progress. Sometimes I had setbacks, but they also seemed to strengthen my program. Joining AA was not the easiest thing I've ever done, but I've never felt so comfortable being sober before. Thanks AA.

Tom F.
Fort Bragg, California

# TRADITION FOUR

Each group should be autonomous except in matters
affecting other groups or A.A. as a whole.

————————— ♦ —————————

*Wherever two or more alcoholics are gathered to practice
AA principles, they can call themselves a group.*

There are all kinds of AA groups—big groups, little groups, off-beat groups. Groups that welcome beginners with coffee and cookies, groups that prefer a warm handshake and a smile before the meeting begins, saving refreshments for later.

Guided by the spirit of autonomy—"a ten-dollar word," as Bill W. calls it—each group is free to manage its own affairs, fitting its customs to the alcoholics it serves. Like the many freedoms AA offers to individuals, autonomy allows an AA group to be whatever its members want it to be, so long as it doesn't affiliate itself with anything or anybody else or do anything that would greatly injure other groups or AA as a whole.

As the writers of the following story, "The Group Conscience in Action," relate regarding their home group in San Francisco—a special purpose meeting supported by the local central office—"We were everything an established group should be—but we weren't autonomous!" Putting the question of autonomy up for a vote, the group conscience propelled the group to stand on its own—"much as a pigeon might tell his sponsor he was ready to stand on his own feet ...

"We now feel we are truly a group and not just a meeting ... Our group's new attitude—knowing just who we are—has made us feel very much a part of the sober structure of Alcoholics Anonymous."

# Personal Conduct and the Group
August 2013
(Grapevine Online Exclusive)

Although autonomy is a $10 word, in relation to us it means that every AA group can manage its affairs exactly as it pleases, except when AA as a whole is threatened. Is it true we have no rules in AA? Using my personal experience as an example, my sponsor tells me I should:

- Get to the meeting early enough to get my refreshment and be in my seat before the meeting starts.
- Pay attention during the meeting. Refrain from whispering and messing around.
- Count the money in the basket after, not during, the meeting.
- Keep my comments brief if the secretary/chair has stated, "Please keep your comments brief."

What is this all about? Well, my sponsor was more than happy to explain. Applying the principle of Tradition Four to myself, for example, I see that I am autonomous except in matters affecting other people in my group or AA as a whole. I can act however I choose in a meeting as long as it doesn't affect the group negatively.

When I behave in ways that are distracting, I may block the message being heard by a fellow member. If I am leaving the room during the meeting, talking to someone, or coming in late, the person next to me or sitting on the other side of the room may miss what is being said.

At my home group, during the Friday night meeting in Libertyville, the conscience of the group was to include this statement at the beginning of the meeting: "In support of AA's singleness of purpose, we ask that you keep your comments confined to alcoholism and limit them to three minutes."

Apparently, what I say at the meeting when it is my turn to share affects other people in the group. It is my responsibility to do the best I can to refrain from talking on and on and to speak about recovery in AA from alcoholism. Not only does it conform to the principles of Tradition Four, but also Tradition One, which is our unity. So, part of "carrying the message" is in my behaving well in meetings.

Can I apply this principle to my work group, family group, or another group of which I am a part? Well, I certainly aim to.

Linda W.
Lake Bluff, Illinois

# Bare-bones AA
May 1992

When you're unhappy with your home group, how should you handle it? Stage a revolt? Grumble and moan? Form a faction and engage in guerrilla politics? Stay on, even when it's apparent that the group conscience has left you behind? None of the above are constructive to serenity or good AA. But there's another choice: Quietly depart from the group, and start a new one.

That's what a dozen or so of us did five years ago after our long-time home group—I'll call them the Whiz Bangs—had strayed down paths that we didn't want to follow. It was a strong group, with many longtime sober members. But a cadre of devoted, non-rotating officers, plus a handful of my-way-or-the-highway bleeding deacons, had locked the group into a format that robbed its former upbeat atmosphere.

The meetings alternated between dictatorship and anarchy. After each meeting opened with the moment of silence, the Serenity Prayer, the Preamble, and "How It Works," the secretary took up to 10 minutes with rambling announcements. By then it was 8:20. When the members broke up into four subgroups, you couldn't be sure whether chairpersons would be on hand for each one. Cross-addicts—many of them dropped off at the door by our local rehab centers—were allowed to engage in grassalogs and cokealogs. The treasurer insisted on keeping $600 or more in cash reserves at all times.

Am I describing inferior AA? Not at all. The Whiz Bangs had a right to set their own policies. The group was—and still is—well-attended. But for a few of us, the former magic was gone. So we quietly split. Sometimes it's better to switch than fight.

We found another meeting place on a different night of the week, and established a closed discussion group with a bare-bones format. It may not be mainstream AA, but it seems to work for us.

We start at eight o'clock. We close at nine sharp. We try for 55 solid minutes of discussion in-between. One way we achieve this is by eliminating non-vital announcements and "How It Works."

We open with the Serenity Prayer and the Preamble, to which we tack on these words: "This group has determined that our discussion will be limited to AA, alcoholism, and sobriety. We therefore ask that you please refrain from references to addictions other than alcoholism." This cuts out the grassalogs without actually discouraging attendance by cross-addicts (of whom we have several).

The discussion doesn't open until someone volunteers, loud and clear, to chair next week's meeting. The chair must provide his or her own subject. We have zero tolerance for the "Does anyone here tonight have a problem?" nonsense, which allows thousands of AA discussion meetings to be derailed by members who think a love spat or burned toast are suitable topics.

We welcome visitors. Same for AA newcomers, but we don't devote entire meetings to them. You'll understand why, if you've ever seen a brand-new member—usually hungover and shaking—subjected to an hour of preaching by a roomful of old-timers who think they're inspiring the new guy with details of their own recovery.

We don't give out chips or birthday cakes, either for newcomers or old-timer anniversaries. We hold infrequent business meetings and short ones, at that. Offices rotate often. The set-up person has light duties, and for one month only. But if he or she doesn't show, or fails to get a substitute, there is unshirted hell. It's happened only once since our meeting was founded.

We're a small group, but we outdo some of the larger ones in the size and regularity of our contributions to intergroup, to the General Service Office, and to the church where we meet. In some ways we sound hardline, but our meetings are friendly and usually filled with laughter. We enjoy AA, sobriety and each other.

After we left the Whiz Bang Group, many of its members looked on us as traitors. But now some of them are drifting into our meetings, and like it. We have no argument with the Whiz Bangs or anyone else. We're neither the best AA group around, nor the worst.

We're just a small band of men and women who were out of step with an established AA group, and who elected to move on rather than stay behind and play dog in the manger. The end result was a plus for everyone concerned.

Anonymous
Indian Rocks Beach, Florida

# A Matter of Tradition
April 2004
(From *Dear Grapevine*)

Perhaps no Tradition is more misunderstood than the Fourth Tradition, which states, "Each group should be autonomous except in matters affecting other groups or A.A. as a whole." The letter "Public Meeting Lists," in the January 2004 issue [describing an intergroup's decision not to list closed AA meetings in newspapers] is a perfect example. No intergroup, area, or GSO for that matter, has the power—thank goodness—to tell a group how they should or should not be published in newspapers or websites. Each group has the freedom to choose how the meeting is run, how group funds are disbursed, and whether and how the group should be listed in newspapers.

If we disagree with a group's conscience, we can always find or start another group, (which I have done). If a group does not abide by our Twelve Traditions, it will surely die on its own. Sometimes quickly but more often slowly.

Paul V.
Grants Pass, Oregon

# The Group Conscience in Action
December 1977

We would like to share our group's experience of transition in structure, because it has given us renewed strength and hope through our growth. It's sort of "what we used to be like, what happened and what we are like now" at a group level.

Our group was a long-standing, closed, speaker-discussion meeting that followed AA guidelines and Traditions. That is, we conducted it according to the pamphlet "The AA Group" with the approval of the group conscience. We had an able steering committee and rotating officers, including general service, Grapevine, H&I (hospitals and institutions), and intergroup representatives. Many regular members considered our group their home group, and we had a good mix in quality and quantity of sobriety.

We seemed to be staying sober and carrying the message by bringing our recovery and sobriety to AA service through group unity. Those present felt they were attending meetings where the genuine hand of AA was extended. You might think we would be grateful as a group, given all this, and have serenity as officers and members.

Yet we were frustrated, especially those of us on our steering committee. We were everything an established group should be—but we weren't autonomous! For a long time, our group had been a special purpose group and had been sponsored by our central office. We were self-supporting, yet we gave all contributions (above refreshment expenses) to the central office. It, in turn, paid our rent and gave us our literature. Yes, we felt uncomfortable. Though we had good sobriety and a sound group conscience and meeting conduct, we felt we were treated like a newcomer who still had to lean on a sponsor.

So our members and officers moved, through our group conscience, to become an autonomous group—much as a pigeon might tell his sponsor he was ready to stand on his own feet. We wanted our structure to reflect all of the Twelve Traditions, especially the Fourth ("Each group should be autonomous except in matters affecting other groups or A.A. as a whole") and the Seventh ("Every A.A. group ought to be fully self-supporting, declining outside contributions").

The way we achieved our autonomy was as important to us as our decision to try. It took a few months of putting our group conscience "into action" for us to receive the rewards of "how it works."

We put the autonomy question before the steering committee and the group for a vote, and received group-conscience approval. We then took our proposal to our local service committee for recognition and approval, which we received.

Now that we're autonomous, we pay our own rent, as well as continuing to buy our own refreshments. We have a group number in the records of the AA General Service Office, and we order our own literature from AA World Services and our own group subscription from Grapevine. We handle our own contributions, following the "60-30-10" recommendation (60 percent to our central office, 30 percent to GSO, 10 percent to our area general service committee).

We now feel we are truly a group and not just a meeting. Nothing has drastically changed in our meeting conduct or our ability to carry the AA message. But our group's new attitude—knowing just who we are—has made us feel very much a part of the sober structure of Alcoholics Anonymous.

We've brought our individual recovery to sober action through group unity. We feel it helps the Fellowship as a whole each time a group matures this way. We've done a thorough housecleaning and taken a group inventory. Our informed group conscience is no longer frustrated, for it can now act autonomously on the decisions it reaches. We've put principles before personalities and the AA Traditions before local customs. Autonomy has made us feel more assured that the door we hold open to the alcoholic who still suffers (and that's the long-timer as well as the newcomer) is the true door of AA recovery and fellowship.

To be sober members of an autonomous group in the Fellowship of Alcoholics Anonymous, we are truly grateful.

H. A. & J. M.
San Francisco, California

# From the Bottom Up
April 2008

This morning, as I was reading the book *Thank You for Sharing—Sixty Years of Letters to the AA Grapevine*, I came across letters in a section regarding a story about the Lord's Prayer in AA meetings. As I read from letter to letter, each opinion voicing valid concerns and viewpoints from both sides of the issue, it occurred to me that there may be no better reason for AA members to learn the Traditions and our service structure, and how they allow us to operate, than this topic. It is virtually as old as our Fellowship itself, and returns as regularly as clockwork.

Personally, I have never felt the need to argue about whether or not the Lord's Prayer belongs in AA meetings, because I know that the Fourth Tradition tells me that "Each group should be autonomous except in matters affecting other groups or A.A. as a whole." Therefore, I know it's the group's choice to recite this prayer and not some proclamation that came down from on high.

But change in AA does not occur from the top down, and a letter to the General Service Office in New York is not a letter to the "powers that be." Besides, regardless of how much or how well we write, all GSO staff is going to do is reply that they support the group's autonomy and they leave the decision where it belongs, in the hands of the individual members. AA's service structure is inverted, and any changes in AA come from the Fellowship and from the groups themselves.

In other words, we can write all the letters we want, but if we don't like something that is going on in our AA meetings, regularly attending group business meetings is one way to begin changing it. Once in the business meeting, we begin to see how the group functions, how our Traditions work, and how the service structure ticks. Reading the pamphlet "The AA Group" will give a better idea about how everything meshes.

If we feel strongly about a topic, we can bring it up in the business meeting. A motion may or may not get passed. But one thing is for sure, we'll see where the power in AA rests: on the shoulders of each member who feels strongly about a topic and seeks to change or defend it. We'll also be less likely to be drawn into arguments about it again, too. Safe in the knowledge of how change really happens in AA, we might sit back, listen to the new person's impassioned pleas, and ask, "So, why don't you attend the business meeting next week if you feel that strongly about it?"

Dave R.
Manchester, New Hampshire

# When Prayer is a Problem
October 2000
(From *Dear Grapevine*)

Some thoughts on saying or not saying prayers of whatever religion in AA meetings:

Group conscience and the group autonomy described in the Fourth Tradition are important and powerful principles, which have contributed greatly to the success of the AA Fellowship. If a group conscience is to say the Lord's Prayer or some other prayer, it obviously does not affect other groups or AA as a whole, since there are atheist groups, agnostic groups, and, of course, groups whose members are from religious backgrounds other than Christian.

When I find myself in an atheist group or a group saying a prayer in a religion other than my own, I pray that I will be able to feel only respect and love for the people of that group and their right and need to express their beliefs and faith.

Robert B.
Surry, Virginia

# Kid Stuff
March 2001

I was sitting in one of my favorite closed AA meetings when I looked up and saw two children in attendance. I immediately began to get uncomfortable. I told myself to remain calm, keep an open mind about this, and get what I could from the meeting. Well, there was no hope for it: I just couldn't ignore those children flapping around in their sandals, making repeated visits to the coffeepot, going in and out of the door, and whispering with their mother.

I am a teacher and, now that I am sober, very active in community affairs. So I am uncomfortable with the possibility of these children turning up in my school or some other place in the community and breaking my anonymity. (Adults have trouble with that concept; we can hardly expect children to understand it.) I was also angry because these children created distractions during the meeting. And I was in conflict with my desire for their mother to stay sober and my own needs. I really resented being placed in this position and wanted someone else to do something about it.

Then I got out of my self-centeredness and started thinking about the children: How must it feel for them to have to sit still and be quiet for an hour? Five minutes of that is a long time for a child; an hour is an eternity. Should we expect little folks to do something so foreign to their development? Is it fair to them? Many of us have spent so many years being misguided parents, shouldn't we think about how the children are feeling?

I mentioned the incident to other alcoholics from other groups and found out that most groups had had at least one experience with children coming to closed meetings, and they had come up with a variety of solutions. Some groups provided (and paid) a baby-sitter to watch the children in another room during the meeting. Other groups allowed children to stay as long as they were "good." However, everyone had a different definition of "good," a different tolerance level for children, and a different idea of what to do if they weren't "good." Furthermore, attendance had fallen off at some of these meetings. In another area, sober mothers got together and took turns baby-sitting, so that they could all go to meetings without having to worry about their children or about disrupting anyone.

Not wanting anyone to dislike me, I kept all of this information to myself and avoided closed meetings where I knew that children would be present. At the same time I was harboring a resentment because no one had "straightened these people out." But as with most things, the problem came home to roost. Children started showing up at my home group, and I could no longer avoid the issue. I would have to take a risk and say my piece about children attending closed meetings in a group conscience meeting.

It wasn't as bad as I thought; we felt sure that we would find the answer in a Tradition somewhere, and we did. We decided that closed meetings were for those who have "a desire to stop drinking" and unless the child had a drinking problem, he or she shouldn't be there.

End of story, right? Wrong. Some folks with children took a dim view of our decision and went off to bad-mouth our group. Well, so be it. As Tradition Four says, "Each group should be autonomous except in matters affecting other groups or A.A. as a whole," and we are being guided by that.

Ruth Ann H.
Waldorf, Maryland

# Let Them Buy Cake
July 2010
(From *Dear Grapevine*)

I n response to recent i-Say Forum comments about Seventh Tradition money being spent on food or medallions: Groups are autonomous. In my group the members donate the food and we buy a cake, because we are enjoying ourselves. We have fun, something we never could have dreamed of when drunk.

Bill W. wrote a great editorial on group autonomy in Grapevine ("On the Fourth Tradition," March 1948), which also appears in *The Language of the Heart*, a book I lean on to help me see AA life through his eyes and to remember that AA doesn't need me to police it.

Alcoholics Anonymous grows and flourishes, as does my humility. I need to focus on being a trusted servant to others.

Anonymous

# A Question of Safety
April 2002

"I don't feel safe," someone at a meeting will share, or "Let's keep AA a safe place." And I will think, Safe from whom? Safe from what? Safe from the outside world? Perhaps, but it is more likely that the world needs to be kept safe from me should I pick up a drink, given my drinking history. Safe. Sometimes the word seems to float lonely, unattached, through the room, seeking a context. Sometimes, hearing the word, I feel, well, unsafe.

I noticed that the business meeting that normally followed the regularly scheduled meeting on the first Thursday of the month did not take place. The next month came and again no business meeting. The same thing the following month. I asked the chairperson about it. "We have business meetings when we feel like having business meetings," he said. I went to another member of the group. "We're not into business meetings," he said.

The group began to seem different. A group officer wandered around with the collections from the previous three weeks seeking to know who the treasurer was. The chairperson's personality seemed to intrude more on the meeting. Vacancies in some service positions went unfilled. The offerings on the literature table looked sparse. It became difficult to share simple things about sobriety at the meeting: the premium seemed to be on wit over sincerity.

Then, at the group's monthly anniversary meeting, the celebrants shared their gratitude for their year or years of recovery. At the secretary's break, the elderly manager of the center where we met asked for a few minutes of the group's time. She spoke with pain and anger. She said that we weren't cleaning up after ourselves. She said that time after time the meeting place was being left in disarray: chairs weren't put away, garbage was not disposed of, the floors weren't swept and mopped. She said that some group members, when she sought to discuss the problem, gave her the runaround, that they tried to con her with flip answers. "Keep it up and I'm going to put you out of here," she announced to the stunned group.

Each group has the right to be wrong (and the right to be right). Tradition Four tells us so. And yet, among the sweetest words I hear at any AA meeting these days are, "There's a business meeting following our regular meeting tonight. All group officers are asked to attend, and members of the group are encouraged to do so as well." A regularly scheduled business meeting increases the probability of group unity, of an informed group conscience rather than the whims of a few. It increases the probability that group officers will, along with the right to serve, have a sense of responsibility regarding their service commitment. A business meeting is a way of saying that we as members have a right to an accounting of our Seventh Tradition contributions with a treasurer's report. It is a way of allowing the general service representative, through his or her report, to introduce into the consciousness of the group the idea that the group is not an end in itself but part of the service structure beyond it. It is a way of ensuring that we take our inventory so our hosts won't have to. It is a way of saying we care.

Safe from each other and safe for each other, and safe for the person coming in behind us, the alcoholic who still suffers—that is what I think safe means. Safe through our Twelve Traditions from the irresponsibility that was such a feature of my active alcoholism.

David S.
New York, New York

# TRADITION FIVE

Each group has but one primary purpose—to carry its message
to the alcoholic who still suffers.

———◆———

*No matter how different we may be, we are bound
by one common goal.*

Doing one thing supremely well rather than many things badly is advice Bill W. offers through this Tradition. Bound by
our obligation to the alcoholic who still suffers to carry the
message of recovery and hope—something each AA member can do
simply by virtue of sharing his or her own experience in getting sober—each AA group has a singular responsibility that animates everything it does.

When we first come into AA, many of us—often down on our
luck—are secretly (or not so secretly) hoping that AA will be a sort
of lending establishment, an employment agency or even a housing
authority. But before long, we recognize that what the group has to
offer is far more valuable than any of these things: a way out of the
misery we are currently mired in.

"If there is any one thing on which all, or nearly all, AAs can
agree, maybe our primary purpose is it," writes B.L. in the story
"The Challenge to Ego in Tradition Five." "We do not have to see
eye-to-eye on theological issues, on politics, on the causes and psychology of alcoholism, or even on how to stay sober. So it is beautiful, I think, for us to have one notion we all salute and honor—our
primary purpose. When we carry the message to the alcoholic who
still suffers, it binds us together and can heal ever so many wounds."

# Let's Get to Work
May 2013

Our group thought we were a model AA group, so it took us a while to notice that we just might be failing at our most important job—to carry the message to the still-suffering alcoholic. But around that time, the theme of the San Antonio International Convention, "A Vision for Us," had sparked a months-long discussion among our members that ultimately re-focused our group conscience on becoming more relevant to the world of alcoholism around us. The process was not exactly a group Fourth and Fifth Step, but we did get a good, long look in the mirror and, as a result, a chance to do a better job.

It all started on a beautiful late summer day in 2010 with a few of us gathered at the ranch of a long-sober AA friend to hear about the San Antonio Convention from some of our group members who had attended. Stories of the huge crowds of AAs, fantastic speakers and fellowship on such a scale created a sense of belonging to something big and important. As we discussed the state of our own group, we could not help but take some (you guessed it) pride.

After all, in the five years since we had established the group in our blue-collar mill town in the southern Rockies, we had grown to more than 40 members and had given our community a valuable new resource. People were getting sober. Our veteran members were passing the message to newcomers with energy. Cordial and useful personal relationships were being forged all the time. Our reputation among AAs in the southern part of our state was on the ascendant. The group was coming together and the thought that we might not be carrying out our primary purpose was the farthest thing from our minds.

But the more we talked about the encouraging message to groups from San Antonio, the more we questioned whether we were really doing all we could. The contrast between the success our members were experiencing and the worsening alcohol and addiction scene in our community was unsettling. We started to wonder whether we were becoming less like the shining city of sobriety on a hill and more like an Alamo full of self-satisfied drunks on the mend. We decided to do something about it.

Our point of departure was staying sober ourselves, so we doubled down on Big Book and "Twelve and Twelve" studies and sponsorship. Then we turned outward. One member's job took him to rural parts of our state, so we armed him with extra Big Books and other AA materials for struggling groups out there. Another member with a connection to the health care community wrote an article that was published anonymously in a medical journal about how we alcoholics hide from our doctors and what doctors and nurses can do about it. We reached out to our most remote state prison with a subscription for 24 Grapevines. When one of our members moved back home to Ireland, we set up a corresponding relationship with her new group there and started sending our favorite AA books and pamphlets their way.

We broadened our celebration of Founders' Day to include special attention to the role played by women like Marty M., Sister Ignatia and Lois W. in AA's early history. We now host an open meeting honoring the AA women pioneers to which we invite wives, mothers and sisters of members to recognize their part in our recovery. Recalling the vital work done by AA staff in New York to get the message out nationally, we invited our members during November Gratitude Month to contribute $2 to GSO for every sober year they had. We recently sent in a grateful $503 to New York and intend to do even better next year.

Is all this just pride on a group level? We hope not. We are simply trying a little harder to reach outside our group to attract the still-suffering alcoholic in the same way that we had to get out of ourselves to connect with the group in the first place. Tradition Five says, "Each group has but one primary purpose—to carry its message to the alcoholic who still suffers." For our group, that has meant going into action beyond our circle of sobriety. We have embraced carrying the message of AA to alcoholics both in and outside our group and, in doing that, may have found a true "vision for us."

Bill H. & Alec H.
Pueblo, Colorado

# Stormy Weather
September 2013
(From *Dear Grapevine*)

I recently celebrated my 36th year of sobriety. I had always assumed the Fifth Tradition was meant for newcomers. I used to have a narrower view of "the alcoholic who still suffers." I love being sober, but sometimes a sober life is like sailing on the ocean: One moment the day is sunny with a steady breeze, then 20 minutes later, a stormy gale. Fear and doubt can creep into my brain as the boat rises and falls in mounting waves, making me pray for the blinking harbor lights.

Just because I have years of sobriety doesn't ensure me against storms. I too can become the "alcoholic who still suffers." I too have the right to raise my hand and talk about the fears that disturb my soul.

Time in sobriety can become a trap. What will the newcomer think of me? Will my friends think I'm in for a fall? Sharing my fear today— no matter how much time I have—is an act of courage that makes my sobriety stronger.

Tim Mc.
Marietta, Georgia

# A Benevolent Guardian
May 1994

When I got to this Fellowship, I knew nothing about it whatever. I only knew I hurt and I wanted to stop hurting—but without stopping drinking. After all, alcohol was the solution to my problems. It made life bearable. But for some reason I stumbled into a meeting and heard AAs tell their stories. They didn't look like drunks, but they certainly talked like drunks. I felt at home—without having any idea why I felt that way. I know now, of course. It was because these people had obviously been where I was, had thought what I was thinking, and had felt what I was feeling. I belonged there as I had never belonged anywhere in my life.

I was told to keep coming back, so I did (in those days I wasn't asked to come back anywhere very often). I went to a group that met only once a week and occasionally I would honor it with my presence. I had no intention whatsoever of stopping my drinking. I would drink, get more depressed, and invariably phone the central office—about 2:00 A.M. I remember the hour only because that's when the bars closed. Someone would talk with me while I told my long, woeful drunken stories. Of course, I wouldn't tell the little group I attended that I was drinking constantly. Why bother them with little details like that?

I was constantly in a fog, but one night I was driving aimlessly around, extremely drunk and depressed, when it suddenly popped into my head that "my" group was meeting at that very time. It had been in progress for half an hour. I staggered in, blind drunk. Nobody was very surprised. The meeting continued while I sat drunker than a skunk. After the meeting they took me out to coffee.

One night during the meeting, a "hard core" member said, "There are people sitting right here who are coming to this meeting and drinking all week." He looked straight at me. I almost went through the floor. (Note: That man later became my sponsor.)

It was after that meeting that I learned about the Third Tradition. Other members of the group said to me privately, "Marion, you want to get sober, don't you?" I said, "Yes." They said, "Then you are a member of this group if you say you are and nobody can throw you out." They quoted the Third Tradition. I said "Put me down as a member," and so I became a member of Alcoholics Anonymous—permanently. But I kept drinking. Nobody ever said I had to be sober to be a member. I wasn't.

I continued to phone the central office, and several times it sent Twelfth-Steppers to see me. Strangely enough, it was members of my group who kept making these Twelfth Step calls. Why did they have to come when I called for help? I still didn't want the group to know I was drinking. On one of these calls, three people from my group arrived at my apartment (they knew the challenge I presented). I told them to take my bottles. It took all three with arms loaded to carry away my liquor. (I always wanted to have enough to serve my guests. Of course, I never had guests.) That night I took my last drink.

Several months into my sobriety, I found out that my group had made a project of answering the night phone for the central office: it was these members who'd been listening to my long and woeful drunken tales. They knew all the time—everything! I was aghast. It was bad enough that they had picked me up and taken me to meetings, taken me out to coffee, befriended me in every way possible, and finally convinced me, beyond doubt, that I was suffering from a progressive and fatal disease. To think that they had been listening to my monologues through the wee hours of the morning added insult to injury.

Unquestionably, that group had been conspiring against me to get me sober. I felt it had violated my privacy and somehow infringed on my constitutional rights. I was most unhappy that they knew me from top to bottom. I hadn't wanted to be known. I was afraid that if they knew me they wouldn't like me. It took a long while before I understood they both knew me and liked me, and that I was OK just as I was.

Then one day I really heard the Fifth Tradition. It jumped out and hit me like a bombshell: "Each group has but one primary purpose— to carry its message to the alcoholic who still suffers."

It sounded like a bugle call. It marched right off the page, and I thought, Dummy, that group wasn't meddling in your affairs or infringing on your privacy. It was, and is, a spiritual entity carrying out its primary purpose. Don't you see?

Of course. I see now. This single primary purpose stands as a benevolent guardian over every group, everywhere.

Marion D.
Albuquerque, New Mexico

## The Teddy Bear and the Tradition
May 2002

An incident at a women's meeting brought the importance of Tradition Five to light for me. When the secretary asked if there were any AA announcements, a woman with a few years of sobriety announced that she had flyers for a women's retreat and that those interested could see her after the meeting. When she finished, a woman with loads of time in sobriety blurted out, "That's not an AA announcement!" The whole room went quiet. I noticed that the faces in the room revealed many emotions, but the most common was confusion.

At our next meeting, I talked with the secretary. She had called our central office about the validity of the statement and received contradictory responses. We truly did not know if announcing a retreat for women was AA or not.

A few days passed, and the question kept bouncing around in my thoughts. I decided to call Jane, who had spent most of her sobriety in and around district and area meetings. When I explained what had happened at the meeting, I heard her chuckle. She said that she could not tell me whether what the woman had said was right or wrong, but that she had a story that would help me to understand the situation and to make my own decision.

At her home group, there was a woman who made teddy bears. She decided one day that she had too many and so she brought them to a meeting to be given away during the raffle. (The raffle is a common event at most meetings in the Northeast and consists of people buying tickets to win Conference-approved AA literature and bumper stickers.) At the next business meeting for this group, the elders informed the woman that she could not contribute teddy bears to the raffle because only Conference-approved literature could be given away. There was a vote and it was decided that the teddy bears, no matter how cute they were, had to go. Even though the nos were a majority, my friend Jane felt it was neither a clear nor a good group conscience vote.

A few weeks passed and Jane went to the district meeting. The woman with the teddy bears and the others who had voted against the majority had brought their dilemma to the district. For some reason, the district felt this was a group issue and decided to let the group decide, which gave the woman and the others, in their minds, the OK to distribute teddy bears during the raffle.

So, the teddy bears were ready to be raffled at the next meeting. At this meeting was a man with some time sober who had come with a woman who was two days sober and at her very first AA meeting. The woman won the raffle (of course) and the man handed her a Big Book. She was not impressed and informed him that she wanted a teddy bear instead. The man told her that the teddy bear was not going to keep her sober. She insisted that she really wanted the teddy bear. The woman left the meeting with the teddy bear. She was never seen again, but the teddy bears still remain.

Jane's example helped me in understanding our Fifth Tradition. It was a simple message that I could bring back to my home group. From that point on, we have tried to be very careful what we include in our AA announcements and raffle.

When I came to AA, I did not know that drinking was my problem.

A teddy bear might have seemed, in my sick mind, an easier, softer way to solve my problem. I could have been the woman who did not come back. We never truly know what newcomers will hear at their first few AA meetings that will help them to stay sober, but we can be responsible for what we make available to them, so that they can get the help they need to understand the disease of alcoholism.

Kathi A.
Acton, Maine

# One Primary Purpose
August 1997
(From *Dear Grapevine*)

I have been meaning to write to Grapevine for a long time and I guess the article "Pass the Tissues, I've Got Issues" gave me the motivation to do it. As a recovering alcoholic, who happens to be a gay male, I can't stress enough the importance of gay special-interest meetings, in addition to non-special-interest meetings. This is partly due to some of the very issues brought up in the article. An important part of my recovery has been the ability to tell my story, unabridged. Due to my own character defects and my perception that there are prejudices in the world, I find this difficult to do at non-special-interest groups.

Tradition Five says, "Each group has but one primary purpose—to carry its message to the alcoholic who still suffers." I would like to say that this is true at gay as well as non-special-interest meetings that I attend.

Jim S.
Maryland

# The Challenge to Ego in Tradition Five
November 1976

Over coffee at an all-night cafeteria some years ago, disagreements flared among four or five tables of AAs. There was dissension about the bookkeeping of the clubhouse treasurer, about dues and rules for membership, about the brand of coffee, and about the right of the program secretary to schedule a nonalcoholic speaker. I recall feeling vehement about several of these matters, and I expect I got loud, too.

Suddenly, someone brought to our attention a newcomer who had attended his very first meeting that night. All arguing ceased, as if by magic. Everyone pitched in to comfort Charlie and encourage him. Even those of us who did not care for each other acted polite and friendly, for new Charlie's sake.

We ended the evening amicable and united. Although this happened in 1945, before our Twelve Traditions were written, their good sense prevailed among us. It was a beautiful demonstration that "Each group has but one primary purpose—to carry its message to the alcoholic who still suffers," our Fifth Tradition. No one doubted that Charlie's welfare was more important than our petty arguments.

For me, there was still another lesson embedded in that one. Since I was so new myself, I had been made to feel very much like the most important alcoholic present—until then. But when Charlie appeared, I wasn't. Not even to myself.

Much later, I realized that my nose had not gone fiercely out of joint, that I had not gone all-over jealous. I had been so eager to help Charlie (with my vast store of AA knowledge gained in about six weeks) that I had not suffered even a twinge of sibling rivalry. I began to think of someone else, not of what I wanted.

It was a classic illustration of the "twelfth suggestion" made in the book *Alcoholics Anonymous* at the beginning of Chapter 7: "Practical experience shows that nothing will so much insure immunity from drinking as intensive work with other alcoholics. It works when other activities fail."

So the Fifth Tradition, like the Twelfth Step, encourages me to become progressively less self-concerned and more concerned about others. Traditions repeatedly have that effect on me, and that is why I rank them as highly significant in our process of recovery.

The Fifth, like others, has a liberating effect. As AAs, we don't have to get tied up in owning real estate or operating clubs, with all the organizational, legal, and financial hassles and ego battles such projects would involve us in. We need not try to become a medical or a religious fraternity, an educational organization or a political one. Because of the Fifth Tradition, we are free of the necessity of raising large sums, or trying to change society. It is not our purpose as AAs to educate children about drinking, nor to teach the medical profession or the government about alcoholism. These might be side effects or spin-offs, of what we do, just as a network of enjoyable and therapeutic social activities may also result from AA life. But they are not our chief purpose; they are subordinate to our goal of staying sober and helping others.

Another time, I saw AA members really mistreat a sick and shaking alcoholic. He had managed on his own to get to the clubhouse where the group met, and he asked for somebody to talk to him—to tell him what he should do to stay sober.

No one had time. Clubhouse officers had to discuss the upcoming anniversary party, and a couple of other members were planning new furniture arrangements and swapping fishing tales. My excuse was that I was just a visitor from out of town and had to catch a plane home soon.

I felt awful on the flight and took our inventory pretty sternly. It was the clearest instance I could remember then of violation of our Fifth Tradition.

We all agree, I hope, that such things should not happen. Aren't we unanimous in the conviction that helping a new prospect is more important than planning a party or chinning with old friends?

If there is any one thing on which all, or nearly all, AAs can agree, maybe our primary purpose is it. There's a world of things we can all disagree on, thanks to Tradition Five. We do not have to see eye-to-eye on theological issues, on politics, on the causes and psychology of alcoholism, or even on how to stay sober. So it is beautiful, I think, for us to have one notion we all salute and honor—our primary purpose. When we carry the message to the alcoholic who still suffers, it binds us together and can heal ever so many wounds.

B. L.

New York, New York

---

# Are We Forgetting Why We're Here?
May 1994
(From *Dear Grapevine*)

I had an experience this week which I want to throw open to discussion. One of the groups I attend had its Christmas potluck supper on a meeting night. I invited a homeless, male alcoholic to attend this function with me. He declined. This chap has been in treatment twice and was in AA for a year back in the 80s. He recently had four and a half months of sobriety, though he had more or less been drunk since late October.

As I was leaving for the potluck supper, he showed up at my door. He agreed to come along with me, knowing that I was in charge of some of the preparations and that we would arrive an hour early. He sat in a small room off the kitchen, smoking and waiting while I did my chores. He had been drinking, but was not in a loud, obnoxious state. He does look like a street person—unkempt and dirty.

As the AAs arrived I explained that "Bill" was by himself. I asked two of the men to spend time with him. They did—a short time. No one else approached him. As these well-dressed, sober AAs continued their festivities, Bill sat by himself. When dinner was served, I went to get Bill. He was out in my car saying he felt he didn't belong there.

Has AA forgotten its Fifth Tradition? Has it gotten so involved with roundups, dances, potluck suppers, picnics, and workshops that it has lost sight of its primary purpose?

I did my best to tell Bill that all those people inside are alcoholics— we are all the same. However, my weak explanation made less of an impact than those AAs ignoring Bill. Both of us left.

I admit Bill is difficult. But I'd like someone to tell me why he should want to be an AA member.

J. H.
Thunder Bay, Ontario

# Sobriety to Go
May 1992

As often happens, we learn the most in AA from listening to our newer members, and my home group recently experienced a new dimension of the Fifth Tradition because of it.

We have a periodic group inventory every four to six months, so that we can stay healthy as a group. We use the Traditions as well as some of the questions from "The A.A. Group" pamphlet as our guide. We pick a separate night and spend three or four hours checking our group pulse. At one of these inventory sessions, we had gotten to the Fifth Tradition when a member who had been with us for five months or so spoke up.

"I am confused," he said. "This Tradition says that 'Each group has but one primary purpose—to carry its message to the alcoholic who still suffers.'" He paused a moment, then hesitantly said, "I have been attending this group recently for five months now, and we have never left this room!"

The result of this new member's wisdom and willingness to participate is that our group now sponsors a weekly meeting at a local treatment center. We carry our format and our group's message to them. From this weekly Twelfth Step activity, our group has grown as some of the alcoholics in the treatment center join with us when they leave treatment.

Our group has benefited in several ways other than new members. For a while, we saw an influx of nonalcoholics into the AA groups. Many of these came to us from treatment, having been told to just go to AA by well-meaning professionals who were not really familiar with what AA did and did not do. We have learned that we were at fault when this happened. If we do not show up to explain AA to new people, they will hear about it from people who do not know about AA.

This simple activity of carrying the message out of our meeting room also answered another problem we were having. Those of us who have been blessed by being in AA when there were plenty of "live" Twelfth Step calls talk a lot about them. Our younger members now have an inexhaustible supply of "live" Twelfth Step calls.

By regularly showing up at the treatment center in the spirit of cooperation, we are getting to know the professionals who do deal with problems other than alcohol. When someone shows up at our group who needs help of a different kind from that which we deliver, we can direct them to a person who can help, rather than just throwing them into the winds. This helps us in our effort to stick to our primary purpose, helping alcoholics achieve and maintain sobriety.

By being willing to stick close to our primary purpose, by being willing to actually carry the message physically out of our meeting space, we as a group have made our statement—if you attend a meeting at our group, you will hear the message of Alcoholics Anonymous, and if you watch us, you will see the message of Alcoholics Anonymous in action.

By being a member of a group that participates in the Fifth Tradition as an activity as well as an idea, I find myself more aware of what I was taught from the beginning: The Traditions apply to my personal life as well as to my group. Just as the primary purpose of my AA group is to carry the message, as a member of AA, my primary purpose also is to carry the message. I may not always like the little sacrifices of time and effort, but I am never confused as to what saving my life by God was really all about. The Twelfth Step and the Fifth Tradition make it clear that my sobriety is not only for me—it is for you. Thank God I belong to a group that acts the same way.

Don P.
Aurora, Colorado

# TRADITION SIX

An A.A. group ought never endorse, finance or lend the
A.A. name to any related facility or outside enterprise, lest problems
of money, property and prestige divert us from our primary purpose.

———————◆———————

*Entanglements can overwhelm our purpose and
keep us from carrying the message.*

Helping alcoholics recover is what we do best. However, from time to time, some of us get ambitious and feel there's more that we ought to do. Bill W. describes some of the notions early AAs had for expanding on our primary purpose and getting involved in all kinds of enterprises:

"It occurred to us that we could take what we had into the factories and cause laborers and capitalists to love each other. Our uncompromising honesty might soon clean up politics. With one arm around the shoulder of religion and the other around the shoulder of medicine, we'd resolve their differences. Having learned to live so happily, we'd show everybody else how. Why, we thought, our Society of Alcoholics Anonymous might prove to be the spearhead of a new spiritual advance!"

Experience has shown, however, that AA groups aren't especially well-suited to handling outside projects. And even on a personal level, AAs can get pretty tangled up trying to fix things they have no business being involved in. Writes John G. in the story, "Enthusiasm Unbounded," "At first, it took me a while to see how a Tradition that deals with specific issues—money, endorsement, lending out the AA name—could apply to my own recovery. But the more service I've done ... the more I've come to realize how this Tradition really helps our Fellowship to keep it simple."

# Enthusiasm Unbounded
June 2006

I was a little over a year sober when I began answering phones with my sponsor at our local intergroup. During one shift, he overheard a conversation in which I waxed poetic about the virtues of AA and then tried to help the caller with other problems. After the call, he calmly asked, "Have you ever read the Traditions in the 'Twelve and Twelve'?"

My only exposure to the Traditions had been grumbling attendance at a few Traditions meetings. "No," I answered.

"Well, if you are going to do more service," he said, "you might want to read about them. They're kind of ... important."

Although I was insulted and defensive—my first reaction to many of his suggestions—I realized that he had about 20 more years of experience than I, so I'd better take the suggestion. I'm so glad I did. I loved reading about the trials, errors and misadventures that the early AAs had while developing the Traditions that guide our Fellowship today. I realized that early AAs were just as fallible and, occasionally, as misguided as anyone else. But by returning to our primary purpose, obstacles could be overcome, and the Fellowship would survive.

As I've continued to do service at the group level and beyond, I've witnessed how our Traditions help the Fellowship navigate through all sorts of situations. It's not always pretty either, so I really started to appreciate the wisdom that came from the experience of those in the early days.

One Tradition that I've grown grateful for is the Sixth Tradition. At first, it took me a while to see how a Tradition that deals with specific issues—money, endorsement, lending out the AA name—could apply to my own recovery. But the more service I've done over the years, the more I've come to realize how this Tradition really helps our Fellowship to keep it simple.

For a number of years, I took an AA meeting into a detox every other Friday night. The detox is part of a hospital and is run, like many hospital detoxes, by a trained professional staff. Early on in my commitment, a patient showed up after the meeting started. She apologized profusely and began telling me why she was late. I realized that because I was leading the meeting, some detox patients might assume that I work for the hospital.

I told her that I appreciated the apology, but it wasn't necessary. From that point on, I made sure I explained, at the beginning of each meeting, that I was neither a member of the hospital staff, nor a professional in the field of alcoholism treatment. I told them that I was simply a drunk, just like them, who found a solution in Alcoholics Anonymous. The speaker and I were there to share our experience in the hopes that it might help another alcoholic—we wanted to give back what had been so freely given to us. We had nothing to do with the hospital, we weren't there to enforce any rules, make money, or sell anything. I found it helpful to make this clear from the beginning, both for the patients and for myself. It helped define the meeting's primary purpose, and it also, perhaps, made it easier for the patients in the detox to see me as a peer, not as a counselor or a doctor.

In my own recovery, Tradition Six reminds me not to overstep my bounds. As my sponsor witnessed that day at intergroup, there are times I get excited and try to fix things I have no business fixing. Whether I'm answering phones, talking to a newcomer at a meeting, or working with a sponsee, my only purpose is to share my experience, strength and hope, and to carry the message to the alcoholic who still suffers. There are plenty of competent professionals, more qualified than I, who can handle everything else.

John G.
New York, New York

# Voting for God's Will?
September 2000
*(Excerpt)*

T wo years sober, I was my home group's secretary and in charge of our literature. Always a bookish guy, I added new pamphlets and some French translations to the Conference-approved stuff displayed on our table. I also added two paperbacks about alcoholism from the self-help section of our local book store. I'd enjoyed them, they sold quickly, and the people who purchased them were pleased. So I added a few more.

After three months, the book table at the meeting was half commercial publications and half Conference-approved literature. They were easy to distinguish. The commercial literature had bright, eye-catching covers and arresting titles, some about other addictions, Al-Anon issues, alternative approaches to sobriety, and counseling. The AA stuff was all monochromatic, with block letter titles.

I was having fun, people were amazed at the variety, books were selling, and one person even suggested we ought to rename the meeting "The Book Meeting." Boy, was I gratified to hear that.

Then Frenchy, who had 10 years, leaned over the table one night and said, "I don't remember the group voting to sell non-AA literature. Did I miss a business meeting?"

"Voting?" I thought he was joking. "People love this stuff. Raffle ticket sales are up because winners can choose anything off the table. We're making money. Everybody's happy. What's to vote?"

I heard out his arguments that by carrying commercial literature, we were affiliating the group with non-AA enterprises and taking money from General Service, which is funded in part by the sale of Conference-approved literature. "We're autonomous, and have the right to do that," Frenchy said. "But the group makes those decisions, not the secretary."

Him with his 10 years and fancy talk! He didn't see how much my group appreciated all I'd done. "You want a vote? Fine." I called a business meeting the following week. I'd show this guy.

I could see from the interest when I announced what the meeting was for that it would be well-attended. And I was sure the tide of opinion was with me. So I was surprised at the meeting to hear several long-timers voice the same concerns Frenchy had, and was dismayed to see the cowed, pensive looks when I presented the facts about our growing treasury, and how people sought this meeting out because of the variety of books I'd provided.

When the vote in favor of retaining only Conference-approved literature tallied 26 to one, I was ready to quit. Where were the compliments and support now? This was exactly what I always believed would happen by trusting group decisions: people tell you one thing, then when the chips are down they do another.

My sponsor counseled restraint of tongue and pen, and praying for acceptance. I kept my mouth shut, continued half-heartedly as secretary, but felt hurt and angry, as if this were something they'd done to me.

In the "Twelve and Twelve," Bill W. wrote a dozen years after the fact that, when his group told him that working AA for a fee at Towns Hospital would put the Fellowship in jeopardy, "The group was right and I was wrong."

I don't know how long it took him to recognize that. It took me a few years before I could look back at my own little venture into commercializing AA and say the same thing. Despite their interest in the new books, the group voted in the best interest of AA. They were right and I was wrong.

Today I see that the group conscience overcame in a loving, generous way the shortcomings of the individual—me. I've voted about enough other issues since then to have witnessed how this process absorbs and dissipates the self-pity and resentment drunks like me are capable of nurturing. So I trust that a group striving to live by spiritual principles will achieve a better, higher wisdom (if less than perfect) than I can on my own.

Since I've always been a results-oriented, show-me kind of guy, I must also admit that the long-term results of these group decisions—preserving the Fellowship—have convinced me that they are indeed the expression of a loving God.

Ernest S.
York Harbor, Maine

# A Divorce with Dignity
July 2008

Nearly 12 years ago, on a hot July night, I crawled into my home group meeting. I was almost three years sober and in the middle of a divorce. I didn't want to be there. It was Traditions night. What could I possibly hear at a Tradition Seven meeting that would help with my confusion and fear during this tumultuous time of my life?

The speaker was an old-timer. Bud began by saying that Tradition Seven went hand-in-hand with the two Traditions before it. He reminded us that Tradition Five speaks of the group's primary purpose, "to carry its message to the alcoholic who still suffers." I wasn't listening very intently. I was in self-seeking mode, focusing on myself and my divorce.

When Bud began discussing Tradition Six, however, the words "money, property and prestige" caught my attention. These were the very things I was attempting to retain as a result of the divorce. I sat up excitedly in my chair, finally ready to listen.

A funny thing happened to me as Bud discussed Tradition Seven, however. A group "ought to be fully self-supporting," he read, "declining outside contributions." Wait a second, I thought. Fully self-supporting? Although I understood how a group of Alcoholics Anonymous could be self-supporting, it was a strange concept for me personally, especially in the midst of my divorce. I listened intently through the rest of the meeting, hearing how other members of my home group interpreted these Traditions and how they had applied them to their lives.

As I drove home from the meeting that night, Bud's talk began to take shape in my selfish little mind. Wasn't I seeking money, property and prestige? Wasn't I expecting my husband to provide me with those things as a result of our divorce?

As a result of the Tradition meeting that night, my fears were fading. I was developing a new plan and a new understanding of my part in the problem. My primary purpose was to stay sober and to carry the message to other alcoholics, I reminded myself, not to squeeze as much as I could get out of a divorce. And the only way I could stay sober was with the help of my Higher Power.

What could divert me from my primary purpose? Problems of money, property and prestige! The very things I was seeking were the very things that could divert me from sobriety and a relationship with God. The Tradition doesn't tell us how to obtain money, property or prestige. It states, rather, that seeking these things can present problems, deadly problems.

Finally, Tradition Seven gave me explicit instructions. I am to be fully self-supporting, and not only fully self-supporting, but declining outside contributions. I began to understand what Bud explained to my group that night. God would take care of me. All I had to do was practice the principles in all my affairs, let go of the divorce, and trust that God would provide exactly what I needed.

As a result of showing up at my home group that night and listening to the discussion about Traditions Five, Six, and Seven, my divorce was a spiritual experience for me and for my husband as well. We didn't argue. We divided our property fairly and honestly. We walked away from our marriage with dignity and respect for one another, remaining to this day, almost nine years since the divorce, good friends.

Bill W. wrote the Traditions for the groups, but this alcoholic can certainly learn and grow by making them a part of my life.

Connie E.
Oklahoma City, Oklahoma

# This Is AA
June 2009

In thinking about Tradition Six I'm reminded of my friend George. In the fall of '94 I was on our local intergroup call list. Late one evening, I was asked to give George a call, as he might want help. George said that he had tried "AA" before but it had never worked— during several previous stays in treatment, he'd gone to meetings there. It was a great surprise to George when I said that most of those meetings were run by the facilities; they were not AA groups but a function of the treatment center or hospital. I said I would be glad to meet him and show him the program of recovery that worked for me—as outlined in our book *Alcoholics Anonymous*—and introduce him to an AA group.

Because of the amount of alcohol George had consumed, I suggested a medically supervised detox. After that, I agreed to meet him at my home group. Unexpectedly, I had to leave early, so I arranged for George to be met by a fellow member, Jimmy D.—who became George's sponsor.

Eight years later, when Jimmy D. died, George talked about the wonderful way of life Jimmy had shared with him. George and I often reminisced about how he had given up hope of finding sobriety, and how he thought he had tried AA but had never been introduced to the program of recovery.

"While an AA group may cooperate with anyone, such cooperation ought never to go so far as affiliation or endorsement, actual or implied," AA's Sixth Tradition, long form, says. (AA's Third Tradition, long form, adds: "Any two or three alcoholics gathered together for sobriety may call themselves an AA group, provided that as a group they have no other affiliation.")

Mike M.
Fort Wayne, Indiana

# Friendly Yet Different

June 1990

How can we help alcoholics stay sober in the age of multi-addiction? I've come to believe that cooperation but not affiliation between AA and such organizations as Cocaine Anonymous or Narcotics Anonymous can help alcoholics stay away from that first drink—and live. AA's policy of cooperation but not affiliation with churches, prisons, other fellowships, medical societies, treatment centers, hospitals and so forth may be found in the long form of our Sixth Tradition. (The long forms of the Traditions are given at the end of the Big Book or the "Twelve and Twelve").

A few years ago, a "pigeon," whom I'll call Pete, got drunk. I don't know what happened to him: he may be alive and sober; he may be alive; he may have died drunk. Pete's habit of always talking about his "drinking-and-drugging" allowed him, I believe, to cling to what our Big Book calls a lurking reservation: "I can't drink-and-drug, but maybe I can drink."

About the same time that Pete got drunk, a young lady came from another state where she had been active in Alateen and Narcotics Anonymous. Sue came to a closed AA meeting. Her position was: "I'm not an alcoholic, I'm a drug addict. But I have a desire to stop drinking, because if I drink it will reactivate my addiction to other drugs." Based on what Sue said about herself, and my understanding of how the short and long forms of the Third Tradition fit together, I asked her to please leave and come back to an open AA meeting. She did and she didn't "shoot up" or "get high." Later on, I worked on projects with Sue and other NAs in the spirit of cooperation but not affiliation.

It was a real privilege to visit schools and junior high schools side by side with NA members. I introduced myself to the vice-principal, for example, in this way: "Hi. I'm a member of AA, visiting the schools today. Here's some of our literature that could help a kid with a drinking problem, if you'd care to have it. Here's our phone number for more information." My young friend said, "Hi. I'm Eddie, from Narcotics Anonymous, visiting the schools today too. Here are some of our pamphlets that could help a kid who has a problem with drugs other than alcohol. Our number for more information is here." We didn't plan it, but I wore a business suit while Eddie wore "mod threads" and an earring. We presented a visual image of being friendly with each other, yet different, separate.

My experience has been that since we took great pains to stress cooperation not affiliation in this and many other similar projects, not even the gruffest, gnarled old-timer snarled at us about so much "cooperation." I've helped organize AA workshops with as many as six other fellowships at a time participating as "guests"; registrations for each fellowship were separate and Seventh Tradition baskets ("self-supporting, through our own contributions") went to whichever fellowship conducted the particular meeting. Attention to details, such as separate rooms and different typefaces on flyers, has also been very helpful.

Ninety-nine percent of the newcomers in the year 2000 may be "double-winners" (alcoholic-addicts). They'll have to face the same basic question, as set forth in the Big Book, that every newcomer faces: Can I handle my drinking problem myself (the hard drinker) or do I need help beyond human power (the real alcoholic)?

As a newcomer, hearing other alcoholics talk about booze helped me decide that I needed help from "a power greater than myself" with my kind of drinking problem. I've come to believe that talk about compulsive gambling, compulsive overeating, other drugs, alcoholic parents, or what happened in the last therapy session doesn't help newcomers sort out the basic question: "Am I a hard drinker or an alcoholic?"

Some people like Pete can still deny their alcoholism by dwelling on their "drinking-and-drugging." But thanks to the growth of

CA, NA, and other programs, it's easier for them to focus on their experiences (possibly very few) with alcohol by itself. Focusing on booze can help newcomers decide whether they have the physical craving for alcohol described in "The Doctor's Opinion" and the mental obsession for alcohol described in the first three chapters of our Big Book. Many like Pete now belong to two fellowships and try to change their focus depending on whether they are attending an AA meeting or a CA or NA meeting. Cooperation but not affiliation between AA and CA and NA helps newcomers to Alcoholics Anonymous stay sober—and live.

Anonymous
Denver, Colorado

# Sign of the Times
June 2015

Our group has been meeting at a clubhouse in Vancouver, British Columbia on Saturday mornings for more than 40 years. It's a solid group with over 50 members, many of them long-timers. On the first Saturday of the month we hold our business meetings. At one of these business meetings, one of our new members pointed out that our group's name—which included the name of our clubhouse—was in violation of Tradition Six. The Tradition states: "An A.A. group ought never endorse, finance or lend the A.A. name to any related facility or outside enterprise, lest problems of money, property and prestige divert us from our primary purpose."

There was much discussion regarding this new member's opinion, sometimes very passionate and at times a little heated. When one of our members pointed out that we could write to New York and ask them what to do, another discussion ensued. At that point we decided to put the discussion off until the next business meeting.

The debate went on for several months. Most members were of

the belief that our group name was not in violation of Tradition Six. They pointed out that no one else had ever questioned the name of our home group. For them it had a special history and shouldn't be changed. To help resolve this issue we did write to the General Service Office (GSO). When the reply came it was very "AA-like." By that I mean that GSO didn't tell us what to do, rather, they shared the experiences of other groups. Most groups in a similar situation did change their name.

After a group conscience we all agreed that it was hard to argue that our situation was any different than the other groups that New York told us about. A final discussion took place before we took a vote, and one member in particular made it very clear that he was not happy about having to change the name. But he said it was "the right thing to do," and he was going to vote for the name change. He reminded us that we must place principles before personalities.

The vote was held, and the name was changed. The following Saturday a new sign appeared at our podium. It was a beautiful sign, etched in wood to replace our old group name. The sign read "The Dilemma Group," and it was made by the member who was most opposed to the name change!

Joe H.
New Westminster, British Columbia

## Facing Our Fears
March 2000

I'm grateful that when I came into AA there were plenty of good examples around to teach me the principles we are to practice in order to change our lives. The man who became my sponsor was talking at coffee one day about how he'd been studying the Twelve Traditions and learning to practice them in his daily life. I was interested and listened to what he had to say, although I really thought the Twelve Traditions had no practical application on a personal level and were certainly for people with more sobriety than I had. I secretly figured maybe someday I would "graduate" to the Traditions after I had "mastered" the Twelve Steps. After all, they came after the Steps in the "Twelve and Twelve."

This man talked about placing the common welfare of his family above his own wants and desires, and of placing the welfare of his employer's business and the team above his own selfish desires for personal success. He explained the concept of self-support in a way that I had not heard before by describing the spiritual principle of recovering alcoholics paying our own way in society. The more he talked, the more interested I became. I began discussing these principles with this man while we began to work the Steps. I didn't wait until after I took the Steps to learn. One thing that he told me regarding Tradition Twelve was that someday one of the toughest things I would have to do would be to stand up for these principles and lovingly place them before the personalities in a whole group and tell them that I felt that they were wrong. He said that I would someday be the minority voice and that I would have to walk through the fear of rejection that plagued me because nobody else would do it for me.

That day did come at a Saturday night meeting I had grown to love. It was full of long-timers and AAs whose sobriety I greatly respected. The format for the meeting is that you receive a ticket when you walk in and the first half of the meeting is a discussion by lottery. If your ticket is pulled you get to go to the podium and share on any recovery topic or experience that week relating to how you stayed sober. The second half is a speaker meeting with a break in between.

During the readings and all the things we do to open a meeting the basket was passed. Then the chairperson announced that a second basket was going around for the Oak Street Center Children's Christmas Party. I was sitting in the front row so he brought one of the baskets to me and one to another person in the front row. It was expected of us to walk the basket around the room to help it get all the way to the back and then to the podium safely. As I took the basket I felt great anxiety and looked at the Twelve Traditions hanging on the wall. Tradition Six seemed brighter than the others. Here was a great cause—children at Christmas. They were our children too, because the Oak Street Center was a clubhouse where AA meetings were held. I suppose it could be rationalized that this was not an outside enterprise, but my heart said it was. A clubhouse is a related facility and the children were not AA members. I handed the basket to the guy next to me and said, "I can't participate in this."

The anxiety was growing as I felt I had to do something about this. But what? I am a people pleaser in the extreme. If I said something, I feared these people would tell me I was out of line and I wouldn't have their approval. Nobody else seemed troubled by it as I watched money dropping into the basket.

As I stewed over the dilemma, the meeting began and went on as usual. However, God had a plan for me this night and my ticket number was called. My palms were sweaty as I stood up because I knew what I had to do. I had to stand up in front of a room full of longtime sober people, whom I greatly respected, and be the one to say that this was wrong. I said a quick prayer on my way to the podium. When I got there I took a deep breath and did it. I don't remember exactly what I said but it was very well received ... until the break. At the break I was approached by several members of the majority who tried to "educate" me, told me that I was mistaken, and began sharing their perception of the truth.

In the light of all of this wisdom freely given to me by well-meaning old-timers, I did not change my vote or my mind. What actually happened is that I began a dialogue about the issue and the group conscience eventually decided not to pass a second basket for outside causes.

Several spiritual principles were interwoven into this situation but I owe the entire outcome to God. He prepared me by helping me become familiar with Tradition Six and how these principles work for our good and the good of the Fellowship. If not for the Twelve Steps I would not have had the faith to face my fear and be a minority voice. I did not yet know of the Twelve Concepts as spiritual principles, but I began to learn of the importance of the minority voice to the good of AA before I knew it was a spiritual principle. All of our legacies are supported by each other. It is never too soon to begin learning and practicing all of the principles in "all of our affairs."

Roger W.
Honolulu, Hawaii

# TRADITION SEVEN

Every A.A. group ought to be fully self-supporting,
declining outside contributions.

———————◆———————

*The spirit of responsibility defines our attitude toward money.*

When talking about alcoholics, the words money and responsibility don't always go hand in hand. Money has led many
of us astray. However, now sober, the idea of paying our
own way opens the door to a kind of growth many of us had never known. "Always, we've had our hands out," Bill W. explains. Yet
through AA's commitment to self-support, "The irresponsible have
become responsible."

We might take a moment to ponder this change, especially the next
time the basket comes around. As Gayle S.R. writes in the story "The
Price of a Drink," "I couldn't count the number of times that I have said
in meetings, 'I am grateful to AA and my Higher Power for not having
to pick up that first drink today ...'

"Why not put the price of that first drink that I didn't have to take
today into the basket?" she adds.

Self-support doesn't just stop with money, however. As members we
are asked to give of ourselves in many ways. Writes Mike H. of Ventura, California, in "Means to an End," "In sobriety, I've known prosperity and poverty. My donations have been large and very small,
sometimes barely nominal. But sobriety requires that I give other
things—my experience, strength and hope as an alcoholic, my time
in service to the Fellowship and other alcoholics. These commodities
aren't measured by the contents of my wallet."

# Thanks, But No Thanks
July 1998

I t was nearing Christmas. One of the letters awaiting me bore the return address of the local parish priest. It was widely known in our little community that Alcoholics Anonymous had helped me turn my life from that of the town drunk to a person anxious to help others. Although I was not a member of his faith, the priest had called me a few times seeking help for members of his parish who had no success taking the pledge.

Before even reading the note in the envelope I noticed a check for $100 made out to our local AA group. The accompanying letter explained it was a contribution the priest wished to make to our small AA group "for the work they were doing." As pleased as I was by the thoughtful gift, I knew Tradition Seven stated that every AA group ought to decline outside contributions. The check, however, was made out to "Local AA Group." The determination on what to do with the money was up to the group, despite my knowing it would have to be returned.

I took the check to the weekly meeting, reading the note from the priest praising our work and dedication. "What shall we do?" I asked the members during the opening business session. I then cited the Seventh Tradition.

"But we can really use the money!" someone said. "We need a new coffeepot and it wouldn't hurt to have some new chairs for the clubroom." Others in the room excitedly made other suggestions of things we needed.

"But the Tradition says we can't accept outside contributions and this is an outside contribution," I reminded the group. "We'll have to return the check."

Soon alternative suggestions flooded the room. "Maybe we could tell him to send it to a treatment center," someone offered. "I don't think we can tell him what to do with his money," someone else offered. "Wouldn't that be a violation of Tradition Six and maybe even Tradition Ten?"

The business session, usually lasting only a few minutes at most meetings, soon turned into an hour-long session testing the thoughtful gift against the wisdom of our founders. Everyone came away from that meeting with a better insight and understanding of the Traditions than they'd ever known otherwise.

The check was returned with a carefully written letter approved by the group, citing the reasons we couldn't accept the gift, and thanking the priest but making no further suggestion. The letter quoted our Seventh Tradition and we included a copy of all Twelve Traditions. Everyone involved had been given a deeper understanding of the Traditions through applying them to the problem at hand—the thoughtful gift from the priest.

There are a few members of that group still active some 20 years later and the group continues to grow. We have a pot that makes good coffee and some extra chairs for newcomers. Somehow we found the money.

Kerry L.
Ord, Nebraska

# The Cost of Coffee
July 2015

I came to AA in 1988. Members in that first meeting told their stories of recovery. They also stressed the importance of putting a dollar in the basket and the many things it covers. I was told that if I wanted a soda, there was a can in the refrigerator and to put 50 cents in for the pop. Coffee was also available, along with a coffee "kitty" to pay for it.

I have attended our area assembly for 20 years, and we've talked numerous times about the problem of not bringing in enough to cover the cost of coffee there. At our last assembly, it was reported that we were short $10,000 in the past 12 years covering the cost of coffee. This money might have gone a long way in carrying the AA message. So we voted to relieve the area from being in the coffee business. Individuals could buy cups of coffee from the hotel where the assembly is held.

On the way home that day, I reflected on the fact that we who attend our assembly are considered trusted servants and leaders. In Concept IX in *The A.A. Service Manual,* our co-founder Bill W. states: "Our leaders do not drive by mandate, they lead by example," and "Good leadership never passes the buck."

I could not ask my home group for more money for the area when we were not practicing Tradition Seven, which states that every AA group ought to be fully self-supporting. The Big Book tells me my problem is selfishness and self-centeredness. I can no longer believe that anyone owes me anything, even a cup of coffee.

AA not only saved my life, but changed it for the better. My sobriety is worth more than I can pay. When the basket comes around, do I give generously or do I find reasons to hold back? When I came to AA, I attended 10 meetings a week for the first year. That meant I was contributing at least $10 a week. Now I may attend two to three meetings a week, but instead of just two to three dollars a week, I should still be putting in at least $10, if not more.

So when someone says the coffee is free, think about what that statement means, and think about what sobriety is worth to you.

Ed M.
Shawnee, Kansas

# To Catch a Thief
July 2013

Over the past 22 years that I've been a member of my home group, there have been several occurrences where money has disappeared—or was stolen, if you prefer. Three or four times the group treasurer, short of funds, had "borrowed" group money to buy cigarettes or coffee or something, with the intention of paying the money back at the end of the week. Over time, the amount owed and the accompanying guilt at not being able to pay the money back created a situation where the person felt so badly that they had to talk to someone, usually their sponsor or the group responsibility chair. It would then be brought to the attention of some of the group members. Since the treasurer couldn't pay back the money, it was suggested that the person use their weekly Seventh Tradition contribution to repay the funds. We let them tell us when the money had been repaid. None of them drank.

In another situation the treasurer took the funds to pay his rent, which emptied the group bank account and dissolved our prudent reserve. When this information became public at our monthly responsibility meeting, some members of the group suggested that the person be forced to publicly apologize at our open speaker meeting. After much discussion, a more seasoned member suggested that since the members of the group had elected the treasurer, that we were responsible. We had elected the treasurer.

That completely changed the tone of the discussion. We, the members of the group, had to be responsible. The other point brought up by this future delegate was the question of what was more important, a member's sobriety or money which could be replaced. That former treasurer is no longer a member of the group, but he didn't drink and is still sober. The group members dug into their pockets and replaced the money.

In another situation, contributions were not sufficient to meet the group's financial obligations. No money was stolen. It was summertime and the money collected in the Seventh Tradition was insufficient to meet our expenses. The treasurer at the time felt that somehow it was his fault, so he started to pay the group bills from his own pocket. When the group found out, we were able to explain that it was our responsibility, not his. He was reimbursed, and we announced to the group that we needed those who could to contribute more. We replaced the funds and created a stronger prudent reserve.

My last example is more personal. My wife was the secretary/treasurer of her district. My son from my first marriage was experiencing his own difficulties in life, and came to live with us out of a juvenile custody facility. He took the district treasury, which my wife had not had time to deposit. At the time, I was the sole breadwinner with two young children plus my son and wife to support, and I was not happy. However, it was our responsibility to replace the money, and we did.

When I first got to AA, I had a lot of loudly expressed opinions on many aspects of the program, most of which I didn't understand. These included the most common ones, such as wanting to be president of AA in recognition of my greatness, wanting to re-write the Big Book to suit my tastes and current language, thinking that I should be able to achieve 20 years of sobriety in two years, and the most popular of all—judging others. My sponsor calls it ego.

In spite of myself, and because of the kindness, patience, tolerance and encouragement of my fellow alcoholics, I have been allowed to make many mistakes in Alcoholics Anonymous. I've gently had my mind opened to other approaches prior to condemning others. There's a reason that we take our time to make decisions in AA. Those who've gone before have seen these things occur. It's how the Traditions evolved.

P. N.
Toronto, Ontario

# Means to an End
July 1998
(From *Dear Grapevine*)

I am probably not the only alkie to come to the Fellowship with a protective coat of cynicism, particularly regarding money. When I heard the Traditions and the words from the Preamble about being "self-supporting through our own contributions," I thought, Yeah, right.

That attitude was erased when I heard my first treasurer's report. (I'd become teachable in the intervening months.) It was delivered by a gravel-voiced man named L.A. He got right to the point: "We had more than $75, so we gave the rest away." I didn't hear another word of his report. My head was racing with the thought, Now, here's a group of 30 or 35 people, pretty much all of whom donate a dollar each week. And when they get more than $75, they give the rest away! And this guy sounds like he's proud of it! I didn't need to hear any more; I'd gotten the message I needed: Nobody's in this thing for the money.

Later, I learned about things like prudent reserves and 60-30-10 plans. I saw how money can be important to us without becoming the focus of our attention or actions. Our donations pay the rent, buy literature, and buy refreshments for the meetings. They also fund our intergroups, the General Service Office, and World Services, the activities that make a cohesive whole of AA, present our face to the world, and allow newcomers to find us.

In sobriety, I've known prosperity and poverty. My donations have been large and very small, sometimes barely nominal. But sobriety requires that I give other things—my experience, strength and hope as an alcoholic, my time in service to the Fellowship and other alcoholics. These commodities aren't measured by the contents of my wallet.

Mike H.
Ventura, California

# Tradition Seven in Action
August 2000

My former home group, the Sanibel/Captiva Tuesday Night Group, was put to a test of this Tradition in June 1994.

Frank I. had been an active member of this group ever since I arrived in Florida in 1989. He led meetings, got the group to put on meetings at a local detox facility, made coffee, handled the collection if the treasurer wasn't there, and was ready to go to any length to ensure his own sobriety and to help the group.

Frank, unfortunately, had been a heavy smoker most of his life, and lung cancer began to assail his body in 1993. Despite his physical maladies, Frank continued to attend the meetings and play as much of a role as his condition permitted. And when he reached the point where he couldn't drive at night, several members of the group, including myself, would pick him up and drop him off. His sharing at the meetings, I remember, concentrated on the gratitude he had for the years of sobriety he had enjoyed, and for the benefits that sobriety had brought him and his family. He also spoke about acceptance of his illness, even when he knew it would be fatal. In his last weeks of life, Frank entered a hospice. When Frank died at age 74 in June 1994, the small church on Sanibel was filled with his family and his AA friends, who outnumbered others by two to one.

A few weeks afterward, the group received an envelope from Ohio, where Frank had lived prior to moving to Florida. It contained a letter addressed to the group and a check for $200 from friends of Frank who wanted him to be remembered by this gesture. Most of us realized right away that accepting such a contribution would conflict with the Seventh Tradition, so we called a business meeting. Our group conscience was that we had to return the money, but we wanted the prospective donors to understand why, and we wanted to suggest an alternative way of remembering Frank. I offered to write them a letter on behalf of the group, and I drafted a response and reviewed it with some other members of the group. We thanked the donors for their gesture and told them how much we missed Frank, too. We then quoted and explained the Seventh Tradition, making it clear that accepting the money would pose a conflict for us. We suggested they donate the money instead to Hope Hospice, where Frank had spent his last days. We sent copies of both letters to Frank's widow, Ginny, so she would know how we had responded.

Frank was a great guy. We still miss him and speak of him occasionally. Our handling of the proposed donation was a wonderful way of illuminating the Seventh Tradition for us, one I often have referred to when this Tradition has come up at other meetings.

Dick N.
Fort Myers, Florida

## Getting the Red Out
April 1982

I collided with the AA Traditions when I was five months dry. The social dropouts in the lower Manhattan neighborhood group whose meetings I graced with my presence twice a week, only because I would die if I didn't, elected me group treasurer. I admired their judgment. I was brighter than ever with each drinkless day and clearly superior to anyone clearly inferior. Noblesse oblige, so I obliged them.

They didn't tell me then that nobody else had wanted the job. They didn't tell me their Second Tradition meant they could ignore what I said if they didn't agree with it. They never even mentioned the nub of their Seventh Tradition, which I've come to call "the treasurer's own." Alcoholics and money don't mix well, they could have warned me then; but at that time, I would simply have thought they were apologizing for the sorry state of their books.

They gave me an antique brown accordion envelope wadded with old receipts, and $53 to put in it, their total worth. A red and black, dime-store, double-entry ledger, kept as if by a scribbling chicken, showed wild swings from gain to loss over four years and a current all-time low. Cash flow was negative. Income was off. Spending was lavish on coffee, sugar, milk, cookies, and cups. But one single gross expense outpaced them all: At the end of each month, almost without fail, in an evident excess of misguided charity, a prodigal sum was squandered on cake, no less, for a member named "Anny."

This group needed smart management! I would cut expenses immediately, leaving "Anny," whoever she was, to the end of the month when she came to claim her cake. I would take her aside then and explain (gently) that she would have to leave if she counted on us for anything more than sobriety.

Back in the kitchen, I set rules: one less quart of milk, one less box of cookies per meeting. Name-brand coffee was out; house labels were in. Cups could be had in quantity at bargain prices if one knew where to shop.

Expenses dropped. The idea of quantity discounts so impressed the group's grocery buyers that one brought in a cut-rate case of 60-watt bulbs that he proceeded to sell to members at cost. By the end of the meeting, he was sold out.

After each meeting, I walked home alone, jangling with change, drunk on power. Neatly, I entered income and expenses for the evening in my scuffed ledger and then, exhilarated by my mind's new ability to retain consecutive thoughts, sat into the night to juggle figures on a desk calculator and draw up projections for the group's future success.

But the reports I prepared for the other officers kept coming back to me, apparently unread. Were they sending me a message? I knew they weren't getting mine. I had advanced a plan to tap a so-far-untouched source of revenue: beginners' meetings. Beginners ate too many cookies, drank too much coffee, and were never asked to pay a penny. Passing them the basket seemed only fair. I decided to take it up personally with a member I had begun to trust. He suggested coffee after the meeting, and I accepted. I had never done that before.

"You know," he said, "anytime I see an AA member climbing the walls about money, I see a person in real trouble." He had misunderstood or, worse, hadn't been listening. So I told him again that without money from the beginners, the group itself was in real trouble; we would never get out of the red. He agreed to discuss it with the leaders.

The basket appeared at beginners' meetings, on the speaker's table. It was never mentioned and never passed, and it never snared a cent. Yes, they were sending me a message, but I wasn't getting it. These people stomped on solvency. Maybe they couldn't handle money, or shrank from its potential. They wouldn't know what to do with a surplus if they had it.

By my seventh month in charge, in fact, we did have a modest reserve fund. I decided to find out what they might want to do with it. I had in mind a savings account. I called for a business meeting. I accounted for my stewardship, then presented my plan: A little nest egg tucked away not only would constrain us to live within our current means, but would mean investment in the future, expanding of itself by five and a half percent even as we watched. Who knew where it could lead us?

One of the food buyers raised his hand. "Maybe that's a good idea. We could save up for a party." The boss of all bosses always sat in the back. He spoke up. To me. "How much money do you have now?"

How often would I have to explain this? I told him again it was $120.

"How much do you pay in rent each month?"

"Fifty dollars"

"What do you send every month to AA services?"

"Right now I'm sending $10 apiece to Intergroup, the Institutions Committee, and GSO."

He rose thoughtfully. "Nobody in this group ..." He struck deeper. "Nobody in this group has any business stashing money. What do you think this is—some kind of a bank? We carry the message, and that's it. We keep what's important by giving it away, and nobody here can afford to forget that! How much were you planning to put in this savings account of yours?"

I had started to shake inside. "I guess about $30," I got out. I had planned on $40.

"I move we take your $30 and send it to GSO, Intergroup, and Institutions. Cut it any way you like. And from here on in, let's up our contributions to them all by $5 apiece." He sat down.

He was trying to wipe me out! They all were! They were voting. All their hands were up! So I raised mine, too.

I was out the door before the chairman could report the vote. I knew what I had to do. I carried out their instructions to the letter, then stayed away.

Finally, I did go back, and there was the cake for "Anny," and I was one of the month's anniversary celebrants. I pinned the corsage they gave me to the red wool dress I hadn't worn in six years, because I'd been too fat. "Believe it or not," I heard myself saying from the front of the room, "I am a member of this group," and they applauded.

A year later, I was chairman of another group. I had a bright idea: "Let's have the beginners take up the collection, so they can feel more at home with the group."

The man who handled the baskets got the jitters. "How can we trust the beginners not to take some of the money for themselves?"

"Listen," I told him, "you can't get uptight about money, or you're in real trouble. We'll just have to trust them. The money is incidental."

I smiled inside when I heard that. I was in the black at last.

C. D.
Washington, D.C.

# The Price of a Drink
July 2008

Whenever I go out to dinner in a restaurant with my husband or friends, I find myself drawn to the drinks section of the menu. I also find myself paying a lot of attention to the advertisements in the window of my local liquor store. Thanks to Alcoholics Anonymous and the hope and strength I found in its rooms, I have not had to take a drink since April 1988, and I am convinced that if I keep on following the suggestions, I will continue not to drink, one day at a time. So why my fascination with the price of alcohol? It has to do with the worth of my gratitude.

When I came into this fabulous Fellowship, I was lucky enough to get sober in a place where almost every time the Seventh Tradition basket was passed, someone explained about taking part in meeting the expenses of the group and helping to carry the message to other alcoholics whenever possible.

Early on, what I could do didn't amount to very much. I was single, barely able to meet my personal living expenses, and had a lot of financial amends to make. Even so, a small glimmer of awareness in my slowly clearing brain realized that, because AA helped me not to pick up that first drink, I was saving myself a lot of money on a daily basis. I didn't begrudge that dollar in the basket.

Several years later, I was doing better financially, not going to as many meetings every week, had gotten very involved in general service, and had watched area committees struggle to do service with the small amounts of money that most groups were able to send. It dawned on me then that there was nothing particularly sacred about "a buck in the basket." After consultation with other wiser women in the Fellowship, I decided to at least put in the price of a cup of coffee for myself and the newcomer with only some lint in his or her pocket.

Now I have trudged a few more years down that "Road of Happy Destiny" and connected a few more dots. I couldn't count the number of times that I have said in meetings, "I am grateful to AA and my Higher Power for not having to pick up that first drink today."

Connect ... connect ... connect. Why not put the price of that first drink that I didn't have to take today into the basket? It makes perfect sense to this alcoholic, since I know that not taking that first drink today has saved me not only the price of dozens more that I would have to chase it with, but saved my life, my self-respect, and a long list of other priceless personal assets that I owe to my sobriety.

So, now you know why I pay so much attention today to the drink list on the menu. Today, it's just another spiritual tool.

Gayle S. R.
Hackensack, New Jersey

# TRADITION EIGHT

Alcoholics Anonymous should remain forever nonprofessional,
but our service centers may employ special workers.

———————◆———————

*While AA's Twelfth Step is never to be paid for, special workers can
help make our Twelfth Step work possible.*

"When I came into AA," writes Paul C. in the story "Forever
Nonprofessional," "I was relieved to find that no one was
being paid to talk to me, give me rides to meetings, buy me
coffee, or help me work the Steps. Professionals had tried valiantly
to help me, but I had a huge chip on my shoulder and was unresponsive to their efforts. I was glad to discover that AA didn't have
a special class of Twelfth Steppers or sponsors."

Questions about professionalism in AA have been around since
the Fellowship's earliest days, with members concerned that other
members might be getting paid for providing services to AA groups
or individuals. Yet, as the author of "Professionalism and AA"
points out, in the book Alcoholics Anonymous Comes of Age, Bill
W. makes it clear that while AA does have to hire people where there
are legitimate jobs to get done, "what is not to be paid for is face-to-
face treatment of a drunk."

Summing up in the article, "Just a Drunk," Jack F. of Aurora, Illinois, notes wryly, "There are professionals who are also alcoholics,
but the idea of a professional alcoholic is far-fetched."

Additionally, he shares, "The next time I feel that urge to 'help'
some poor soul, I hope to remember the meaning of Tradition Eight.
I have much personal experience to share, but a 'learned professional' I ain't."

# The Professional
August 1990

The intellectual arrogance and grandiosity that I brought with me when I first came into Alcoholics Anonymous were quickly and expertly enlisted into what was to become a ferocious, ongoing battle: Me vs. the Eighth Tradition. Ladies and gentlemen, welcome to the royal rumble.

The word "nonprofessional," in AA parlance, means that I ought to act in a way that neither affirms nor implies that I am anything other than a recovering alcoholic in a fellowship of other recovering alcoholics. If professional help is what I need, I should go where such help is available, outside AA. Seems clear enough. Yet, before I was 90 days sober, I had become legal advisor to a newcomer who was in divorce court, instructed another to stop taking his medication that a qualified doctor had prescribed, and counseled two AAs in a lover's quarrel.

I no longer play doctor or therapist and I don't give legal advice, but I still catch myself wondering whether the latest newcomer in my home group is really an alcoholic. On what basis would I question anyone's qualification, you might ask? What else, except my expertise on AA and alcoholism itself.

Sometimes, in my zeal when encouraging newcomers to get involved with the Steps, I talk about them as if they were the be-all and end-all. If anyone had told me, even by inference, that I had to get on with the Steps, I wouldn't have stopped long enough to remark, "What an order! I can't go through with it." I simply would've run like hell.

Sometimes, I complain about the way officers conduct business in my home group and set myself up as the "expert" on our group. There were times when I was so sure I knew everything there was to know about AA history. When speaking from the podium, I would hook my thumbs in my vest like a professional 19th century politician pontificating about the way things should be.

Another area where I am made particularly aware of the Eighth Tradition is in speaking to non-AA groups. I have found myself on panels with experts in the field of alcoholism and have been introduced as an "expert" myself. I make it a point to remember something I was told by a member of our local intergroup public information committee: "We need to maintain our amateur standing." The practical side to being a nonprofessional means I don't have to worry about giving a letter-perfect presentation every time.

Tradition Eight also suggests that our service centers may employ special workers. Some of the experience that helped formulate this Tradition was played out in the days of the Forty-First Street Clubhouse, when members had a hard time distinguishing between Twelfth Step work and office employment. In the early 1940s, this controversy was still new and I can just imagine the faces turning blue with resentment as alcoholics tried to understand that the secretary, for instance, was not being paid to stay sober or to do Twelfth Step work, but to answer the phone, write letters, keep records of business transactions, and so forth.

Newcomers still ask, as I did, why we have paid workers (professionals) in AA. As it was pointed out to me, the staff at our local intergroup office, for example, is not paid to do Twelfth Step work. By opening up and helping keep the doors to institutions and correctional facilities open, by collecting data on local groups and publishing updated meeting directories, along with many other fundamental activities, the intergroup staff is paving the way for Twelfth Step work, it's allowing for Twelfth Step work to happen. Carrying the message of hope and recovery is the real "business" of AA. Attempting to conduct such an enterprise on a solely volunteer basis would be highly impractical.

Sticking close to simple, basic AA principles keeps me right-sized. Every recovering alcoholic at every meeting tells me, whether by word or deed, that non-professionalism in AA is one of the best ideas we ever had. Friends in my corner are quick to remind me of this whenever I get too big for my AA britches. So, in the fight for the heavyweight title, I choose to throw in the towel and surrender to the Eighth Tradition.

This way, we both win.

W. H.
New York, New York

# Forever Nonprofessional
August 2002

The Eighth Tradition suggests that AA remain forever nonprofessional, not that AA members can't be professionals.

Early in my recovery a friend and I drove to a cheap motel to visit a drunk on a Twelfth Step call. After a few hours, this very intoxicated man pulled out a big wad of large denomination bills and began peeling them off, one by one, into a pile in front of us. Astonished, I asked him what he was doing. His slurred response was, "You've been very kind. I want to pay you for your time." My friend informed him that he couldn't buy what we have in Alcoholics Anonymous. I hadn't yet heard of our Eighth Tradition of nonprofessionalism, yet here was a stark example right in front of me.

When I came into AA, I was relieved to find that no one was being paid to talk to me, give me rides to meetings, buy me coffee, or help me work the Steps. Professionals had tried valiantly to help me, but I had a huge chip on my shoulder and was unresponsive to their efforts. I was glad to discover that AA didn't have a special class of Twelfth Steppers or sponsors.

Upon joining AA, I attended lots of meetings and events, read the literature, worked the Steps with my sponsor, began sponsoring other men, and became involved in intergroups and general service activity. Later, I received extensive training in alcoholism counseling and got a master's degree in social work. Now, some 27 years later, I am a social worker with many years of experience working in alcoholism treatment programs, jails, child protective services, medical facilities, employee assistance programs, and the private practice of psychotherapy. When my friends in AA ask me if I work with alcoholics professionally, I smile and tell them that you can't be a social worker without dealing with alcoholics.

When I entered the alcoholism treatment field, the main issue for me was how to keep my professional role distinct from my AA membership. I received a lot of help from the General Service Office guidelines, "For Members Employed in the Alcoholism Field." I've taken special care to develop some practical strategies to maintain this distinction.

For example, when I speak publicly about alcoholism or AA—at a professional gathering or to the media—I don't reveal my membership in AA. When I speak as an AA member—at my home group meeting, an AA convention, or to the media on an AA public information assignment—I don't mention my profession. Maintaining the distinction minimizes the possibility of confusion for the public, other AA members, and me.

Occasionally, AA members ask me to write letters to court on their behalf. First, I clarify which type of letter is being requested. One is on letterhead, and I sign it as a social worker; my AA membership isn't mentioned. The other is on plain paper, and I sign it as an AA member; my profession isn't mentioned.

I don't give my business card to newcomers. It just scares them. Besides, to give an alcoholism counseling or psychotherapy business card to a newcomer at an AA meeting might create the impression that I'm trying to recruit new patients from AA. Nothing could be worse for me, and it wouldn't be too great for the newcomer either. So I had a personal card printed with my name, address, and phone number—no titles, degrees, licenses, certifications, professional designations, or academic affiliations—and this is what I give to new AA members. This practice helps keep me focused on AA's primary purpose and keeps me centered on why I'm at an AA meeting in the first place. It's as much for my protection as it is for the newcomer's.

Being an AA member and working in the alcoholism field can be a little awkward at times. At an AA meeting one night, a young man celebrated his one-year sobriety anniversary by thanking his alcoholism counselor by name—me. I took him aside after the meeting and explained that I attend AA meetings as an AA member, not as an alcoholism counselor, for my own recovery. He quickly grasped my point and was most gracious about it.

Another time, I worked extensively with a company's top management team to effect the hospitalization of a valuable executive sorely in need of alcoholism treatment. One night the treatment center unknowingly bused him to an AA meeting where I was to be the main speaker. When I saw him enter the room a few minutes before the meeting started, I explained to him the difference between the two roles. Everything proceeded smoothly from there. (He retired a few years later and the end of his career was sober and successful.)

One evening a couple came to my office for consultation on a troublesome marital issue. They were AA members and they had an audiotape of a talk I had given at an AA convention, which they listened to over and over again. They knew more about my story than I did! They had way too much information on my personal life for me to provide effective psychotherapy of the type they needed. I referred them to a colleague who could serve them better.

I attended many AA meetings with a fellow AA member, a Catholic priest, who was nationally known for his spiritual counseling of alcoholics. He never wore his clerical garb to AA meetings, wanting to be just another AA member, and he always introduced himself just by his first name when he spoke at meetings. Inevitably though, part way through the meeting, the chairman would ask, "Father, would you say a few words?" It's true that some alcoholis m professionals seek too much of the limelight in AA. It's also true that sometimes other AA members won't let alcoholism professionals just be alcoholics at AA meetings.

Of course, I don't sponsor my patients, nor do I offer alcoholism counseling or psychotherapy to the men I sponsor. When AA members in my group approach me to provide alcoholism counseling or psychotherapy, I diplomatically refer them to colleagues. It's unethical to provide such services to those with whom one has a close relationship.

I'm grateful for that last point, because otherwise not only would I not have a place to go, but neither would the alcoholic colleagues I've Twelfth Stepped over the years. One social worker in an occupational alcoholism program sobered up and joined AA after he told me of his problems with drinking and I invited him to meet with a group of mental health professionals in AA. Another therapist told me it seemed prudent to join AA when his hangovers interfered with the family counseling he was conducting in an alcoholism treatment program. I once hospitalized a marriage and family counselor on a Twelfth Step call when he began bleeding from all the wrong places. He had earlier been arrested for drinking and driving, which was especially ironic since he was an instructor in an alcoholism studies program and taught classes for DUI offenders at the time. I'm grateful that AA was secure enough in its primary purpose to absorb my sick colleagues.

I don't think that AA members who are employed as ethical, properly trained alcoholism counselors return to drinking any more frequently than the rest of the AA population. But if they do drink, the news often travels more quickly due to their heightened visibility in the AA community. I do know that the only thing worse than trying to Twelfth Step someone with a head full of AA and a belly full of booze is trying to Twelfth Step someone with a head full of professional alcoholism knowledge and a belly full of booze. These folks need the same compassion, patience and love as other AA members.

A friend of mine is a psychologist who has been sober in AA for over 25 years. He is a tenured professor at a fine university and has an impressive string of publications in prestigious journals of medicine, psychology and addiction. He has shown me that great intellect and professional accomplishment are compatible with humility, as long as humility comes first. Like him, I try to approach AA as an alcoholic who desperately needs its healing, action-oriented spirituality, not as an egghead who has been educated beyond his intelligence and thinks he's immune to drinking again. I've met a lot of people too smart to join AA. I've never met anyone too dumb.

Throughout all my years in AA and the alcoholism treatment field, I've never kidded myself that alcoholism counseling, psychotherapy, or social work is a substitute for AA involvement. Fortunately, the vast majority of AA members I know who are employed in the alcoholism field lead happy, healthy, productive, balanced lives. They take good care of themselves and therefore they can take good care of their patients and can be available to the people they sponsor. AA members—some of whom are my colleagues—show me how and when to distinguish between my professional role and my AA membership. I'm grateful for their example of how to apply the Eighth Tradition in my everyday life. After all, you can't buy what we have in Alcoholics Anonymous.

Paul C.
Oceanside, California


# Who's an Amateur?
September 1982
(From *Dear Grapevine*)

With regard to Tradition Eight—"Alcoholics Anonymous should remain forever nonprofessional ..."—the opposite of professional is amateur. And the original meaning of amateur is one who does something for love. In this sense, I think most AAs are amateurs, doing what they do in AA out of love for the program and love for fellow alcoholics.

D. K.
South Deerfield, Massachusetts

# Professionalism and AA
August 2004

For years I was confused about Tradition Eight. My first introduction to AA came in a treatment center, where the counselors
were AA members who attended meetings with patients and
even sponsored some patients (including me). I stayed sober only a
year that first time, and later wondered if Tradition Eight had been
an issue at all in that situation.

Fast-forward about 15 years, into the 21st century. I am sober now,
and a member of a home group that studies the Traditions once a
week. What little I knew about Tradition Eight before had come from
the *Twelve Steps and Twelve Traditions*, where the issue is compli-
cated by repeated reference to the Twelfth Step. For example, Bill
says, "Our Twelfth Step is never to be paid for, but those who labor
in service for us are worthy of their hire." The issue is confusing, because earlier in the "Twelve and Twelve," Bill says that "unspectacular
but important tasks," such as "arranging for the coffee and cake," are
"Twelfth Step work in the very best sense of the word." According to
this line of thought, activities such as answering the phone at Intergroup, cleaning up an AA meeting room, maintaining an AA website,
or editing an AA magazine, are clear examples of Twelfth Step work in
the very best sense of the word. However, some AA members are paid
for some of these tasks. So I was confused.

When my group read about Tradition Eight in *Alcoholics Anonymous Comes of Age* and then discussed it, I finally listened to and
learned something about this Tradition. That book says that the early
AA members struggled to figure out the AA viewpoint on professionalism. Bill W. says, "That is where the line finally fell: For face-to-
face treatment of a drunk, no money, ever. But AA does have to hire
people so that it can function where there are legitimate jobs to be

done." In that book, rather than talking about the Twelfth Step, Bill makes it very clear that what is not to be paid for is face-to-face treatment of a drunk.

An old-timer in my group put it like this: "It is AA that is to remain forever nonprofessional. That means that AA (in the guise of a group, Intergroup, sponsor, or whatever) does not pay for or receive money for face-to-face treatment of drunks. Now, of course, any AA member is permitted to get paid by a treatment center for being a counselor. That pay is not coming from AA and is not going to AA, and so it has nothing to do with Tradition Eight. The counselor, who is an AA member, is not being paid to do sponsorship, but rather to do a job of alcohol counseling. If he wants to be an AA sponsor, he does that on his own time."

At last I understand this Tradition, at least for today. Perhaps more will be revealed, but as I see it now, this Tradition says that AA does not pay or receive money for face-to-face treatment of drunks. Consequently, 1) Groups and sponsors of course do not charge newcomers for helping them get sober. 2) Paid AA service workers at GSO and local intergroups do not do face-to-face treatment of drunks while they are on the job. They do that on their own time. While on the job, they refer drunks to volunteer AA members for face-to-face work. 3) Paid alcohol counselors doing face-to-face treatment of drunks are not paid by AA, nor does AA receive money for their work. This situation is not covered by Tradition Eight, since AA is not allied with those treatment centers or hospitals. Individual members who are alcohol counselors are acting on their own, and not as representatives of AA. If they engage in AA sponsorship, they do it on their own time, just like all the other AA members.

Every August, one of the founding members of my group (a real character, who is jokingly said to be our spiritual leader—or is it spherical leader?) says that in honor of the eighth month and Tradition Eight, he is offering a special discount on sponsorship for anyone who needs it. Sometimes people take him up on the offer, but a good proportion of them cancel during the introductory trial period. Of course, this is all said in jest at our meetings, and we get a good laugh out of it. Our group motto is, "We will laugh at you until you learn to laugh at yourself," and we practice that principle in all of our affairs.

Gabriela R.
Lynnwood, Washington

## Pay Them, Not Me
August 2014

Going on Twelfth Step calls, chairing meetings, sharing my story, doing H&I service, working on special committees for AA events, and doing general service for my home group are all types of service work, but they do not by any means qualify as paying positions. However, AA does hire people to perform certain tasks.

While I do work a full-time job and have a life, the truth is that the time I give to Alcoholics Anonymous is an investment in my sobriety. I do not need to get paid, nor would I want to. To be paid would take away from the humbling and spiritually fulfilling aspect of service that I need to stay sober.

The work I do that's not seen by everyone is definitely the most rewarding, such as when I am sitting at home counting envelopes or preparing my report for my home group. It's especially rewarding when I don't feel like doing it, but I do it anyway. This kind of service helps me to learn accountability, discipline and humility, which I often lack. These traits can't be bought.

We're taught in Alcoholics Anonymous that service will keep us sober. We're also taught that no person should make a sole vocation of such work. I actually look forward to retiring and donating a larger chunk of time to AA and general service work.

Now, how about those paid positions in AA? How about the men and women at the General Service Office (GSO) who answer phones for book orders, or the ones who process the countless letters, articles, questions, comments, updates or donations? These activities may be service, and even though it's for AA, these are jobs.

Truth is, these jobs actually help make my Twelfth Step work a lot easier. When I call GSO as a part of a service commitment, the person on the line is helping me to carry the message, via books and other literature. They also sometimes answer questions and share experiences other groups may have had. But in truth, the work they do at GSO is hard work—and they should get paid.

I don't put in an eight-hour day for AA. Sure, in the course of a week I may put in a few hours, but that's my time. Any person who is putting in a 40-hour week to facilitate the running of AA should be paid. Anyone who puts in time carrying the message and working with others and thinks they should get paid, I will pray for!

Jennifer M.
Mobile, Alabama

## Paper Jam
August 2008
(From *Dear Grapevine*)

I want to share with you about the Eighth Tradition. This Tradition, in its simplest terms, says AA should not become professionalized and that our Twelfth Step work ought never be paid for.

Yet, sometimes well-meaning AAs look for loopholes in the spirit of this Tradition. A recent example involved the purchase of an industrial copier by an AA service body, in order to produce copies of its newsletter. The vendor, an AA member, offered to save the service body money. He said members could choose not to purchase a maintenance service agreement, and he would perform the required servicing as a personal contribution. The service body agreed and all went well for a while. However, the copier began to have problems and the AA member became increasingly difficult to contact, much less perform the maintenance. The end result was that the copier became inoperative and had to be scrapped at the expense of the service body. The purchase of a service agreement, though an additional expense up front, would have prevented the unexpected expenses involved when the copier broke down.

In my personal life, I need to be reminded that I am not a professional in AA. My service to AA is my ability to transmit a message of hope. That means I ought not play doctor, marriage counselor, banker, lawyer, or pharmacist.

Woody R.
Stockton, California

# My New Best Friend
August 2013

I started working in mental health and recovery services before I got sober. Since I worked with people who had "worse problems" than I did, I never viewed my drinking as an issue. When I finally recognized how far down I had gotten, I came into AA. I wasn't entirely convinced that I belonged here or wanted the AA way of life, and I became a "two-Stepper." I had admitted I was powerless over alcohol (Step One) and immediately began helping others (Step Twelve). But I wasn't too concerned with the rest of the program.

After nine months without a sponsor, I became just as miserable sober as I was drinking. I knew something had to change. When I began working the Steps with a sponsor, I was able to identify the character defects that had gotten me into a dry drunk and kept me there.

Then I was introduced to the Traditions. I typically avoided Twelve and Twelve meetings due to my opinion that they were boring and the fact that I didn't really know anything about them. (I was still working on my humility and didn't want to appear stupid in a meeting; after all, I worked in a recovery center!) I realized that I had violated a couple of the Traditions fairly regularly. First, I had no personal anonymity. I was still in the phase where I told anyone and everyone that I was in recovery and how awesome it was for me. My husband had to pull me aside when we were planning our wedding and tell me to stop saying I was in recovery, because it made the people at the reception hall uncomfortable. It made him uncomfortable too.

It was the Eighth Tradition that held the secret to my dry drunk. I had thought that I didn't need to do Twelfth Step work because I worked in a recovery center and that was my Twelfth Step work. With some guidance and more involvement in AA, I began to get better. Slowly, I learned how to separate my identities. At work, I stopped presenting myself as an "AA." In the meetings, I stopped identifying as an alcohol and drug counselor.

Just before my second year, my husband and I moved and I had to discover AA in a newer, smaller community. This time, I was a little wiser about not making my primary identity that of "counselor" and did my best to maintain my identity as "recovering alcoholic" when at meetings. My sponsor had started to allow me the privilege of sponsoring, and one of my first sponsees attempted to blur those lines again.

When we would meet to do Step work, she would avoid talking about the Step. Instead, she would start talking to me in a more client/counselor style. As time went on, I started to feel like an on-call counselor and struggled with setting boundaries. With help from my sponsor, I was able to start being firm with my position of "Step work, not therapy." When that sponsee continued to try to engage me as her personal 24-hour therapy hotline, I would say, "How does this relate to your powerlessness?" This was not the response she was after. After a few weeks, she decided to find a different sponsor.

Today, I continue to find more and more ways to experience Twelfth Step work without it bleeding over into my job identity. There are still times when I arrange to take a group of clients to an open anniversary meeting or when I run into a former client at a meeting. The two parts of my identity will never truly be separate. However, I know how to set boundaries with women I sponsor, and I don't identify my AA membership at work. And while I still sometimes talk like someone in the program, I choose not to break my anonymity. There are times when others break it for me, but that is their Tradition violation, not mine.

In order to safeguard my recovery and my career, I have learned to put boundaries in place. The first is that I don't go to meetings or do service work in the community where I work. The second is that I don't discuss clients with other AA members. The third is only disclosing my recovery status to co-workers on a "need to know" basis. The fourth is not breaking my anonymity to clients. The fifth is remembering that I still have to be of service in every way I can, otherwise I'll get drunk. I'm not perfect, and sometimes I slip up, but I keep working at it. I have made Tradition Eight my new best friend.

Megan G.
Prospect, Ohio

## Just a Drunk
August 1992

My alcoholic drinking career lasted nearly 35 years. Drinking led to my becoming a liar and thief, constantly living in fear of being found out. Uncontrollable fits of boozing saw me fired, jailed, dishonored, suffering intolerably, going into hospitals and treatment programs, and AA. With a few variations, I repeated that performance over and over for about 19 years. Over a year of my life was wasted in treatment because no one could see that my real problems were a nagging wife, nasty bosses, and people who were out to get me. My way of asking for help was, "Here I am, turkeys, fix me! If you had my problems, you'd drink too."

I sincerely hope that my final treatment program and AA renewal was in 1978. This time around I was lucky to find a sponsor who was strong on the AA program outlined in the Big Book. That program has a noteworthy track record, so he saw no need to put together a custom-made special-purpose program as I had tried to do so often in the past. His idea of carrying the message was like one beggar showing another where he finds the bread, not becoming their baker. Problems have been constant companions, but I have had a sober and reasonably contented life since I've tried to practice the AA program to the best of my ability (emphasize tried).

Alcoholics are likely to enter AA more eager to hear advice on how to straighten out their personal life than how to learn to live sober, troubles and all, one day at a time. Because we are naturally protective of newcomers, a growing number of AA members are just as eager to offer explicit advice about resolving personal difficulties. In so doing, aren't we putting our work on a service plane, rather than sharing our "experience, strength and hope"? "Working With Others" in the Big Book states: "We simply do not stop drinking so long as we place dependence upon others ahead of dependence on God." I have been down that long road. Here are key lines from "Whose Responsibility?" in *As Bill Sees It*: "... an AA group, as such, cannot take on all the personal problems of its members ... the solutions of all his problems of living and growing rests squarely upon the individual ... teaching and practice of AA's Twelve Steps, is the sole purpose of the group."

The first part of AA's Eighth Tradition reads, "Alcoholics Anonymous should remain forever nonprofessional ..." In general, AAs simply take this to mean that AA is a society of amateurs, that nobody gets paid for Twelfth Step work. But professionalism has a much deeper meaning. True professionals are highly educated individuals such as physicians, professors, psychiatrists, research scientists, and others, not merely people who are paid for working. There are professionals who are also alcoholics, but the idea of a professional alcoholic is far-fetched.

In some AA groups there is no escape from would-be experts on alcoholism, sociology, psychology, pharmacology, or you name it. An AA newcomer who innocently asks a question may be inundated with snap judgment directions and advice from those well-meaning gurus.

A newcomer has no reason not to regard those unqualified AAs as "pros," but disastrous results are possible. I wonder where I'd be today if I had followed some strong advice that led me to seriously consider separating from my wife. She supported me and paid the bills during long periods when I was incapable of working. After a suicide attempt, it was my wife who saved my life. And who in AA is qualified to urge another to discontinue taking medications?

I pray that I will stay humble and not forget that I am just a drunk, sober today through the grace of God and the AA program. The next time I feel that urge to "help" some poor soul, I hope to remember the meaning of Tradition Eight. I have much personal experience to share, but a "learned professional" I ain't, nor do I bake another's bread.

Jack F.
Aurora, Illinois

# TRADITION NINE

A.A., as such, ought never be organized; but we may create service boards or committees directly responsible to those they serve.

————◆————

*Finding the sweet spot between disorganization and getting things done.*

This Tradition can be a puzzler. As Bill W. puts it, "How can we have an unorganized movement which can and does create a service organization for itself?"

Digging into this question, Boyce B., the author of "Behind the Scenes," found an answer to this seeming contradiction. "In early sobriety I discovered AA's meeting book for our greater metropolitan area ... While it was as confusing as a train schedule at first, I was like a kid with a newfound toy, running around town to meetings in a great many unlikely places at all hours of the day and night ...

"A couple years later when doing a weekly stint as a telephone answering volunteer at our intergroup office, I was able to see how the information was gathered, updated and regularly published. The meeting lists hadn't just happened miraculously. They were the result of well-organized effort and just plain hard work. At last I came to understand that while AA itself must never be organized, there were some jobs in AA that need to be well-planned."

Adds another member in the story, "Ninth Tradition," "Since so many alcoholics rebel against authority in human form, we just dispense with it altogether. The first seven words of Tradition Nine say that we have no bosses—echoing Tradition Two. But the last 14 words describe the system and orderliness necessary for our outfit to get things done."

# Behind the Scenes
September 1996

As my life got increasingly unmanageable during the last years of drinking, I withdrew more and more and became isolated from meaningful interactions with others. That this was happening in midtown Manhattan made life all the more lonely. So it was with amazement that in early sobriety I discovered AA's meeting book for our greater metropolitan area.

While it was as confusing as a train schedule at first, I was like a kid with a new-found toy, running around town to meetings in a great many unlikely places at all hours of the day and night. Here was a listing that said a particular sort of AA meeting would be held at a certain time and place, and behold, there it was—and run by drunks that I would guess hadn't always been reliable for keeping commitments. This world was a radically different place from where I'd so recently lived and drunk. A whole different set of principles were guiding these mostly sober folks who, while they seemed pretty laid back and casual, were well enough organized to be there when the meeting book said they would be.

A couple years later when doing a weekly stint as a telephone answering volunteer at our intergroup office, I was able to see how the information was gathered, updated and regularly published. The meeting lists hadn't just happened miraculously. They were the result of well-organized effort and just plain hard work. At last I came to understand that while AA itself must never be organized, there were some jobs in AA that need to be well-planned.

As a member of our general service area, I found myself working on the planning committee for our annual area convention, and saw how AA members find strength in getting together to enjoy the broadest community aspects of our Fellowship. So our convention has become an annual custom that provides much joy in living and sharing. It needs a lot of careful planning and organizing to make it happen and to provide for the needs of an unbelievably diverse range of tastes, spirits and temperaments. The going was not always as smooth as we planned as we did the necessary tasks, but the results were beyond our wildest dreams. And we all stayed sober right through the Sunday morning meeting that closed the event. We had created a committee directly responsible to those who need our services.

Boyce B.
Brooklyn, New York

# Ninth Tradition
February 1971

Two flaked-out fellows were shown in a popular William Steig cartoon a few years ago. The caption was something like "One of these days we've got to get organized around here."

I remember expressing the same sentiment while drinking. I not only said it, I did it. To me, getting organized meant getting things arranged in a highly systematic manner, in preparation for getting them done. (You don't necessarily pay your bills, but you do make a neat list of creditors.) During self-enforced droughts, I would zealously over-organize everything in sight in round-the-clock spurts—only to blow it all later in a flood of ethanol. And so I welcomed the idea of an "organization"—which I supposed AA was—for getting something done about the trouble I was having with my drinking.

I approached AA in Manhattan 26 years ago in total darkness as to how it did things. (How often is it approached any other way?) I guess I expected to find a written constitution, bylaws, dues, and paid sergeants of some kind trained to discipline the backsliders. After all, there was a telephone listing, and I had been invited to come to an office. That sounded pretty organized to me.

But the first members I met unwittingly sowed confusion by using familiar terms in an unfamiliar context. Such words as "member," "join," "meeting," "officer," and "committee" do not mean the same in AA as outside it, but how was I to know that? My confusion grew as I heard and saw AA people behaving differently from each other, saying wildly disparate things, sometimes contradicting each other. Some even drank!

I asked about the president of AA, and they said there wasn't any; yet they had a chairman, a secretary and elections. There was no ritual for joining, they said; yet the secretary usually announced, "If you want to join this group, see me after the meeting." They said there were no musts, but that to do certain jobs one must have been sober at least three months. They insisted they were alcoholics, not ex-alcoholics; yet most never touched a drop.

Obviously, I was seeing only the lowest-grade members of this outfit, I became pretty sure. I kept nosing around to find the generals, so I could get the real score. I never found any top brass.

But despite the vast ignorance of the noncom troops, AA got things done. The telephone got answered; meetings were held, with pre-arranged programs; coffee got served; a book and pamphlets were distributed. So AA must be systematized in some way, I had to conclude. But how? Was there a secret hierarchy of authorities who enforced the statutes by making members do things?

Such were the expectations—shaped, of course, by the experiences of my non-AA lifetime—with which I arrived at the door of the Fellowship. With growing delight, and often chagrin, I have learned how mistaken I was.

Now I am convinced that one sure way to destroy AA would be for us to set up a rigid organization patterned after the non-AA societies we all know. Yet we cannot be a laissez-faire body, willing always to "let George do it." Instead, each of us is expected, it seems to me, to assume enough personal responsibility on his own for the Fellowship to get its major function (Tradition Five) accomplished.

What giant problems our first members faced! They had to find ways to get things done without slipping into either the bedlam of unlimited autonomy or the trap of over-organizing and under-accomplishing. The dilemma could easily have overwhelmed them, in my opinion. Organizing can itself be addictive, my personal experience indicated. It's easy to get so fascinated with the process of organizing that I can lose all sight of what I am organizing for. I marvel that any of the first 10 years' members stayed sober at all.

Tradition Nine describes the masterful solution worked out during the first 10 years of AA experience. Since so many alcoholics rebel against authority in human form, we just dispense with it altogether. The first seven words of Tradition Nine say that we have no bosses—echoing Tradition Two. But the last 14 words describe the system and orderliness necessary for our outfit to get things done.

My personal AA life illustrates both the problem and its solution. Like a tantrum-throwing 4-year-old, I figuratively stamped my foot and refused to pay attention to the Twelve Steps. I mistakenly believed them to be rules for staying sober, instead of a simple description of how our first members actually did recover. After enough slips, however, I saw that in AA I had the freedom to try out, on my own, the Steps suggested as a program of recovery. But I had to make myself do them, because no one in AA could force me to. I tried to be bossy in AA, and I got drunk. I learned to empty ashtrays for the group, and I began staying sober.

A few years back, we floundering fathers of a certain Greenwich Village group found ourselves about to be replaced. To make life easier for our successors than it had been for us, we wrote out what each steering-committee member (trusted servant) had done, exactly how, when and where. (This was before the General Service Office published its excellent pamphlet "The AA Group.") We bound these information sheets in a notebook for our new secretary-treasurer. About three months later, we learned that the group was behind in "gifts" to our landlord (a church) and had not paid its intergroup pledges nor several GSO bills for literature. Swift to find a scapegoat, we turned on Ernie, the new secretary-treasurer, and demanded,

"Why didn't you pay those things?" Indignantly, he told us, "Because I didn't know I was supposed to, and I don't know where to pay them, anyhow."

In my most tolerant bleeding-deacon voice, I said, "But Ernie, exactly what is to be paid, and when, and to whom, is all spelled out for you in that book."

"What book?" he asked.

"That black notebook we gave you."

"Oh, that!" Ernie replied with disgust. "I've never opened it," he announced proudly. "Nobody in AA is going to tell me what to do!" Several chronic beginners tipsily applauded.

That nutty contretemps puts the AA organization problem into a beautiful nutshell, it seems to me. How, on the one hand, do we avoid offending each other with government—which inevitably means giving some members authority over others—and still, on the other hand, escape chaos? As the late Bernard Smith so eloquently put it at our 1970 International Convention in Miami Beach, the answer is in the way our Ninth Tradition insures AA against anarchy while at the same time insulating us against any form of AA government. Ernie, working with the other new officers of the group, later came upon that answer himself.

My fellow group founders and I had had our feelings hurt when somebody had first suggested there might be a better arrangement than our paternalistic one, and the new officers took over. We finally realized, though, that the AA custom of rotation in office can be a healing experience for those who can take it and understand the spirit behind it. Rotation is not spelled out in any Step or Tradition. (Neither are many other good AA ideas, such as the 24-hour plan, going to meetings, significance of the first drink, etc.) But it mercifully helps solve the seniority problem we older members can inflict on newer ones, and I think it is within the spirit of Traditions Two and Nine, if not in their wording.

The genius embodied in the Tradition Nine phrase "responsible to those they serve" escaped my detection for a long time, because it sounded too noble and elegant to be more than a truism. When I worked on some AA committees, however, it came to life for me, and I now consider it an astonishing and challenging notion.

What if those of us who professionally serve others outside of AA— whether we are doctors, taxi drivers, professors, or secretaries—had to report, not simply to some boss or professional association with punishment powers, but instead to our clients? In effect, that is the case with AA officers and committees, isn't it?

Once, an AA committee I belonged to heard of a member who was representing himself as an AA official and collecting money thereby. We instantly launched into a discussion of what to do to him. Think about that ...

It took us an hour or so to realize that we had only the right to pray for him, not the authority to punish him. It was an exciting realization, and I continue to stand in awe of this principle: No matter how much you or I may misbehave, no matter how bad a member one of us may be, there is no one in AA with formal authority to fine us, censure us, or kick us out of the Fellowship. That seems to me a clear implication of both Traditions Nine and Three.

I've learned, too, that I can misuse this Tradition, as I have several others, to excuse my own failings. When I foul up, I can shrug my shoulders and say, "After all, we're not supposed to be well-organized." But that's just a cop-out, I fear; Number Nine does not say we ought to be inefficient, lazy, dishonest, or irresponsible. Of course, the lack of authority in Alcoholics Anonymous can exasperate high-pressure types. I think of one of our most popular AA pamphlets, "What Happened to Joe?" The actual writing and production of it took less than four months. But before that, discussions of it had lasted fourteen years! Interminably, committees worried about whether to do it at all, then about how to do it, what it should say and not say, and on and on.

The process would have been much more efficient if some boss had made the decisions and given the orders. But that is not the AA way. In order to be responsible to those they serve, AA servants work carefully, coolly, prayerfully. An AA pamphlet should be based on such preparation, it seems to me, if it is to represent responsibly the entire Fellowship, as all those published by AA World Services, Inc., do.

If Alcoholics Anonymous were organized the way other outfits are, we could move faster, but would the result be more beneficial to all of us, both present members and those yet to come? For our simple stated purpose, our exasperatingly patient committees and boards are ideal, in my opinion. If we took on additional functions—such as managing buildings, providing shelter or medical services, running cafes—an entirely different kind of organizational system would, of course, be needed.

If we tried to organize in the conventional, orthodox ways, we could well become totally disorganized. If we had to thresh out complete agreement on such issues as rules and authority and power and money, we'd split apart. Instead, we let each man hold his own ideas, discipline himself, and march to his own drumbeat. And in our joint determination to do this, we stay truly united after all.

It has been said that, if we want personal recovery, we owe this to AA's future: "to place our common welfare first; to keep our Fellowship united. For on AA unity depend our lives and the lives of those to come."

B. L.

New York, New York

# A Sense of Service
September 1998

Generally, when we hear the word organization, we think of a situation where there are a lot of rules, and someone with a certain amount of power governs or is in control. Out of curiosity, I decided to look in the dictionary for a definition of the word "organize," and I found that to organize means to systematically prepare or arrange for effective operation. Isn't this what has been done in AA? We have service boards and committees of varying natures that we elect or appoint and who assume responsibility without trying to take on authority, people who, because of a true sense of spiritual simplicity and service to others, effectively carry out the duties of whatever job they are asked to perform.

But this sense of service doesn't only apply at the level of boards or committees. Look at the group and the people who regularly get there early and set up the meeting area, the people who make the coffee, clean up the ashtrays, sweep the floor, and carry out the other tasks just because they know they have to be done. These are only a few examples, but the same principles apply in all of AA, be it at the level of group, intergroup, or general service. As long as we have members who continue to have the best interests of AA at heart and enjoy doing the things that need to be done without any notion of power or prestige, Tradition Nine won't be any problem.

Pinky H.
London, Ontario

## To Those We Serve
September 2013

A fellow AA and I were at a state prison to carry the message to the inmates. Our meeting hadn't started yet, and the women were just arriving. We were short Big Books; I had brought only a few, and the prison had relocated their own small supply someplace inaccessible. A few of the women had their own. To my question, "Do you have a Big Book?" one of the women said, "No, I ordered one but it didn't come yet." Knowing the prison did not take orders for Big Books, I was surprised by her answer and asked from whom she ordered the book. Her response was from one of the AAs who bring in meetings. I bristled a little: placing book orders with an AA? No such thing. We're not organized at that level. As Tradition Nine notes, AA as a whole ought never be organized.

I attempted to explain to her that AA prison volunteers have no mechanism to accept individual book orders. But my explanation didn't make sense even to me, so I stopped. In my own ears, I sounded condescending and preachy. ("Never talk down to an alcoholic from any moral or spiritual hilltop ...") And anyway, the AA member who the attendee was referring to would undoubtedly bring the book next time (that volunteer's dedication to our AA prisoners is second to none).

The meeting began in our usual way—reading "How It Works" and the Traditions. As I listened to the readings, I heard Tradition Nine in a new light. "A.A., as such, ought never be organized; but we may create service boards or committees directly responsible to those they serve." It dawned on me that I was directly responsible to these in-mates: they're the ones I'm serving. Not my group, not the district, not the area. If serving them means taking Big Book "orders," then I can do that. It was the difference between the spirit of vested authority and the spirit of service—the two attitudes seemed miles apart.

I'm grateful for that woman's "Big Book order" and the opportunity to understand a little deeper Bill's purpose in Tradition Nine: The in-mates and I can have a true fellowship.

Karen F.
Los Alamos, New Mexico

# Paving the Way
September 1998

It's always fascinating to learn just how people came to Alcoholics Anonymous. In my case, I looked AA up in the phone book and called our local central office. Thank goodness some service board or committee put it there! The person on the other end of the line took my number and had an AA member call me back for the one-on-one, language-of-the-heart introduction that began my incredible journey in sobriety.

At my very first AA meeting, I was warmly greeted and taken to the literature rack at the front of the meeting room. My greeter selected some of the pamphlets for me to take home. I could relate not only to the AA members but to the AA literature as well. Thank goodness some service board or committee wrote, published and distributed these pamphlets!

Although I only planned to attend one meeting a week, I went to more because I had a car and some other newcomers didn't. One would call and ask if I planned on going to a meeting that night and I'd say yes in spite of myself. So, I picked up a meeting list which helped us find meetings—where and when. Thank goodness some service board or committee gathered the information, printed and circulated this list!

Many of my AA friends—and yours too, I'm sure—found the Fellowship in a variety of ways, and not a few are due to some kind of service board or committee whose efforts facilitate our Twelfth Step work. Correctional, Treatment, and Hospitals & Institutions committees arrange for institutional meetings and bridge the gap between a facility and an individual AA or a group.

In some instances, a doctor or member of the clergy recommended AA to their patient or parishioner; Cooperation with the Professional Community committees most probably paved the way. Some AA members were exposed to a radio or TV program, not necessarily produced by AA but by someone who has benefited from the work of a Public Information committee. All these dedicated endeavors of service boards or committees make our Twelfth Step work possible.

The preliminary work done by AA service boards and committees directly responsible to those they serve (you and me) is invaluable to the future of the Fellowship. I might not be here today if they hadn't put Alcoholics Anonymous in the phone book!

Lois C.
Pittsburgh, Pennsylvania

# A Patron Saint of AA
September 1990

I wish I could tell you that after reading the Big Book and the book *Twelve Steps and Twelve Traditions* I experienced a spiritual awakening and grasped a total understanding of our Traditions. I wish I could tell you that as a GSR, DCM, and an active member of several standing committees, I have never violated the principles set forth in the Traditions. But, typically alcoholic, I gained most of my knowledge and understanding from my mistakes and through the mistakes of others. Sadly, I made most of those mistakes after several years of sobriety when I should have known better.

As a GSR at my home group, I was extremely adamant about Traditions. I tried to dictate moral behavior, told people what literature they could or could not read, and even made violent threats to one man because he was saying bad things about the group. I would run guilt trips on those who refused to get involved with service work while bragging about my own involvement. After about a year of this self-imposed misery, I found it necessary to get back to the basics of AA. I discovered that I had forfeited my own serenity.

Being a slow learner, I found myself gradually slipping back into my old behavior. I was a DCM at the time. Controversy seemed to dominate my AA life. I was constantly engaged in heavy debate with other trusted servants over issues that were none of my business. I justified this behavior by rationalizing that I was preserving the integrity of the Traditions of Alcoholics Anonymous. Today I realize that my behavior was just another example of my alcoholic thinking.

One day as I was reading the Ninth Tradition in my "Twelve and Twelve," a message was suddenly revealed to me that I had never noticed before. Even though I had read that particular chapter many times before, I had never understood its true meaning. I had always thought that it merely gave authority for the formation of a service structure. The new message had an entirely different meaning.

I suddenly realized that I had been trying to impose organization into the Fellowship. In my own way, I had been exacting my own brand of punitive action against those who I judged to be less sincere than myself. I had ordained myself as a patron saint of AA.

In prayer, I asked for forgiveness from my Higher Power. At the next area assembly I was selected to chair a meeting with the GSRs and DCMs. With all the humility I could muster, I made amends to all those present and later to those individuals who had felt the sting of my verbal whip. Finally, again in prayer, I turned my will and the care of AA over to God, as I understand him.

I found the essence of the Ninth Tradition cleverly concealed on page 174 of the "Twelve and Twelve." Bill wrote, "Great suffering and great love are AA's disciplinarians; we need no others."

To me, the Ninth Tradition epitomizes the spirit of anonymity, clarifies the Second Tradition, and provides us with an avenue through which our efforts in carrying the message of AA can have continuity, structure, and cohesiveness. It is the principle that necessitated the foundation of the Twelve Concepts. It requires that I recognize the autonomy of each group, even when I disagree with some of its policies. It will always stand as a personal reminder to me that my service to the Fellowship must come from a space of love. And finally, the Ninth Tradition will always serve as a tourniquet for this once-bleeding deacon.

Charles M.
Columbia, Tennessee

# Round and Round We Go
September 1992

"**A.A.**, as such, ought never be organized ..." In fact, AA at the group level resists organization. There is something at AA's core which keeps it simple and true. In my home group, we have typed up a simple format outlining how to conduct a meeting, and we put it between two sheets of clear plastic. Along with that, we have the Twelve Steps and Twelve Traditions each encased in plastic. All of this is in a file folder which is given to whoever is chairing the meeting.

Over the course of time, these sheets become worn and coffee-stained. And eventually some new member attempts to clean them up, retype, organize!—and in the course of organization, perhaps add some new ideas. But it doesn't work for long. Eventually, the new, clean and "organized" sheets become as wrinkled and coffee-stained as the old, and the group reverts to its traditional manner—keeping it simple.

How attractive and wise this seemed to me when I gathered my courage to attend my first AA meeting. I had expected some kind of formal initiation rite—perhaps religious—and instead I found a group of relaxed people sitting in a circle sipping coffee, actually asking if anyone had an idea or topic. This lack of formal organization appealed strongly to me, because I felt right away that AA was going to allow me to be me—in my own crazy way—and was not going to insist that I accept any views or rules or regulations about drinking or not drinking. I didn't know it at the time, but Tradition Nine was working its spell on me, allowing me to find my own way, through shared experience and love to acceptance and then enthusiasm for our AA program.

I discovered that on the group level, it was the willingness to help one another, the love I saw in action, which served as the real glue that held us together. At first, I thought that the group secretary or GSR or Grapevine representative must be the real bosses of the group. But then I began to see rotation in action, and I learned the difference between ruling and serving. Rotation is one of the ways we use to make sure we serve and don't rule, and that we don't get overly organized. I learned that AA on the group level might seem disorganized or even chaotic to a newcomer, but this was a temporary condition. If the newcomer kept coming back, he or she was soon a member of the group chorus saying, "Let's keep it simple," and "Remember that we are but trusted servants." In such individual freedom is our great strength.

When I began serving as GSR and then DCM, my education continued. Here I saw the need for certain kinds of service structures. We organized an intergroup office and needed a part-time paid worker, as well as numerous volunteers. We set up a Twelfth Step answering service to make sure that an AA contact was always available. It was vital that all this should work well: We wanted the hand of AA out to all those who still suffered.

In setting up these services and making sure they worked well, it was tempting to forget about the principle of rotation and just find some good people and leave them alone to do the job. How much more difficult it was to hold on to rotation and make sure that humility (rather than power-building) was at the center of our efforts. We learned that even though it was more difficult to rotate and constantly have to move through a period of necessary learning, this was good for the individuals involved and for AA. The service committees learned, through hard knocks, to do their job well, and they also learned that no one person, or small group of people, needed to stay in particular serving positions. Our service structure started to hum along with few difficulties, and what is perhaps best of all, many people got a chance to serve rather than just a few.

This same experience proved true as I served on the area level. Here we needed an effective area newsletter, so we could communicate information of importance about recovery. And we needed working committees: Grapevine, Literature, Cooperation with the Professional Community, Archives, Public Information, Hospitals and Institutions, and Finance. How could we get those various jobs done so that AA in our part of the country could be available and unified to those still suffering under the lash of alcoholism? The answer again was to create service boards and committees directly responsible to all members in our area. The strong tradition of rotation serves as a basic spiritual principle, and the work gets done in a spirit of grateful volunteerism. The "organization" in the committees is free and easy; the idea is to do what is necessary in a way that seems comfortable and within all the Traditions. Those holding service positions are the custodians of our AA Traditions; because they do not govern, they do not derive authority from their titles.

I found some of these lessons rather easy to learn, but some quite difficult. For those of us raised in a tradition which suggests that more and more organization is good—and that authority increases as one's title gets longer on the door—AA's tradition of the "least possible organization" and rotation (even if this permits some inexperience and even ignorance) was a bit shocking. Could such a structure stay intact? Wouldn't it finally fall apart? The answer, I discovered, was this: AA is unified and strong, it seems to me, because we are not organized. We have, first of all, always focused on the importance, the dignity of the individual, and second, we've insisted that all those serving AA derive their authority from a loving God expressing himself within the informed group conscience.

The Ninth Tradition, in summary, stands for selfless service in the cause of AA unity. To move along comfortably in the Ninth Tradition is to serve in a spirit of love and knowledge, recognizing that we need not fear, as Bill W. put it, "... blighting organization or hazardous wealth." AA does indeed have a unique character, and the Ninth Tradition, which appears so paradoxical at first, is one of the primary guarantees of that unique and precious character.

Jan P.
Spokane, Washington

# TRADITION TEN

Alcoholics Anonymous has no opinion on outside issues;
hence the A.A. name ought never be drawn into public controversy.

———————◆———————

*Steering clear of outside issues allows us to focus
on what we do best.*

Controversy seems to be a habit with some alcoholics. We just can't keep our opinions to ourselves. Yet in the story, "Fatal Distraction," Jim N. of Denver, Colorado, writes, "When speaking as an AA member, I have no business taking a position on an outside issue, no matter how noble the cause ... By not endorsing or opposing anyone or anything, we are free to concentrate on the one thing we do best, which is to fix drunks."

The author of "Opinions: Yours, Mine, and Ours," got a real-time lesson in AA's position on outside issues as a newcomer. "Early in my sobriety I remember thinking, as I headed to a meeting, I wonder what my newfound friends will have to say about today's events. I can't remember what the events of that day were; maybe some political scandal that had broken or an election ... I could hardly wait to hear what my fellow AA members thought about it.

"The meeting started, a topic was introduced, and the discussion began. No one even mentioned the monumental event of the day. It might have been discussed over coffee later, but it wasn't a part of what was going on in that meeting room."

Wisely, Matt F., author of the story, "The Beauty of Tradition Ten," sums up, "Angry debate of things over which we have no power can only serve to split us."

# Sassy Pearls of Wisdom
October 2015

When I sat down at my very first meeting, I was four days sober and miserable over the wreckage I was causing myself and others. I was comforted to see the Twelve Steps on the wall, but surprised to see the Traditions. I had never heard of them before. When I read them over, Tradition Three made me feel welcome, Tradition Five made me feel hopeful—but Tradition Ten is what really blew my mind. It said, "Alcoholics Anonymous has no opinion on outside issues; hence the A.A. name ought never be drawn into public controversy."

Whoa! What a brilliant idea, I thought to myself. I instantly saw how I could use this in my day-to-day life. Imagine if I had no opinion on outside issues? The wreckage I had made had a lot to do with my big mouth and "edgy" opinions. My life's mission had been to fix everything, because I always knew best. This drunk had all the answers, and I was determined to let you know it. But strangely enough, people weren't grateful for my sassy pearls of wisdom. Who knew that people don't like being talked down to? I always ended up hurting others, and myself, by trying to force my ideas on the world.

I knew my amends list would be long, but I became determined to stop it from growing, here and now. And Tradition Ten was the key. Any time I felt the urge to control someone, I repeated this mantra to myself: I have no opinion on outside issues. It helped me keep things to myself instead of piping up whenever I wanted. Suddenly I wasn't hurting so many people anymore.

Was it hard to practice? You bet. But practice makes progress, and today—three sober years later—I no longer feel the desire to control everything. My way is not necessarily better than everybody else's. I have no business sticking my nose where it doesn't belong. In fact,

I've been using Tradition Ten as another Serenity Prayer, accepting the things I cannot change.

I still love to help people, especially when it comes to carrying the message of AA, but now I know that I can't force my experience on you. I've learned the difference between helping and controlling.

Wendy L.
Vancouver, British Columbia

# Fatal Distraction
October 1992
(Excerpt)

Some months ago, a chairperson closed the meeting by asking everyone to "remember our troops in the Middle East." If this had been an open meeting, nonalcoholics would have gotten the idea that AA supported the Gulf War.

This incident of remembering the troops during the Lord's Prayer made me ask myself: What does Tradition Ten have to do with my personal sobriety and what is my responsibility as an AA member to keep the AA name out of public controversy?

One of the most reassuring things for me about being newly sober in AA was the sense that my private life was protected. Nobody cared how I felt about the Vietnam War, or the Catholic Church, or anything. All that mattered was that I wanted sobriety. At the same time, AA itself had no opinion on any of these things.

Several AA Traditions support this sense of privacy. Tradition Three states that the only requirement for AA membership is a desire to stop drinking. Tradition Five says our primary purpose is to stay sober. Other Traditions support the concept of AA staying out of public controversy. For myself, I can only understand Tradition Ten by seeing how it is related to the other Traditions.

In most other societies there are beliefs, mores, codes of ethics and allegiances that the candidate for membership is required to accept as a condition of belonging. Sometimes these good movements seek public attention and their members receive notoriety. In AA we shun all such personal attention; we stay anonymous. What this does for the new person in AA (as well as for the whole Fellowship) is to give the assurance that the society he or she has joined will never be a source of embarrassment or ever pose a threat to personal privacy.

It is comforting for me to know that the society to which I have entrusted my life would never ask me to pledge allegiance to anything but my own sobriety. Tradition Ten guarantees my right to think, act and believe any way I choose. It also extends to others the right to live as they choose. We don't want to dry up the world or change other people's attitudes about drinking or anything else. We are not in the business of alcohol education or social reform.

Here are some other examples which show how easily we can forget the importance of AA Traditions. Arriving late at a discussion meeting recently, I heard the speaker talking about the amount of alcohol advertising on TV. She was complaining that advertisers had a bad influence on the country's youth by connecting sports with alcohol. She finally got worked up enough to say, "It's up to us to let the world know there is a better way to live and that this alcohol is really evil." The next speaker picked up the same theme and developed it further. Now, no one for a minute believes that Alcoholics Anonymous is going to go on record against alcohol. But if we aren't united about that within AA itself, how can we hope to stay united about it with the general public?

At another recent meeting, the speaker made an appeal to the audience to support MADD—Mothers Against Drunk Driving. Bill W. says in connection with civic responsibility that we have every right to get as involved with social causes as any nonalcoholic. As a private person I can support any cause I like. But when speaking as an AA member, I have no business taking a position on an outside issue, no matter how noble the cause. What if someone at this open AA meeting had gone away thinking that Alcoholics Anonymous supported

MADD? That person, not knowing of our Tenth Tradition, might have gone to the papers and in all sincerity said that Alcoholics Anonymous was promoting this cause. If AA took a stand for or against MADD or any other issue, our singleness of purpose would be lost.

The list of possible controversial topics that could be addressed from the AA podium is virtually endless. It happens now and then that a speaker will try to tie AA directly to Christianity and to suggest that Alcoholics Anonymous itself is a Christian movement. But AA asserts that religious belief is a matter of personal choice. It's in the Big Book. It's in the *Twelve Steps and Twelve Traditions*. And like politics and social reform, religion is an outside issue that could divide AA.

Recently at a meeting a young newcomer approached me with his Bible and other religious literature. He told me that he didn't need AA because he had his Bible. It seems to me that the first half of Tradition Ten works together here with Traditions Three and Five. We don't engage in questions of a person's religious or political affiliation. And because we don't, it wasn't necessary for me to argue with this fellow about his. Tradition Ten gave me the flexibility I needed to be a more effective sponsor. Bill W. says that real tolerance of other people's beliefs and lifestyles makes us more effective in what we're trying to do, which is just to stay sober and carry the message.

What if AA were Catholic, Protestant, or Hindu? What if we had different schools of AA? The new person would first have to decide where he fit into all this tangle of different brands of AA. Then he would have to measure up or down to expectations that have nothing to do with staying sober. At the same time, if Alcoholics Anonymous took a position on any of these things, it would create a fatal distraction for every member, new and old.

The fact is that as soon as a new person comes to AA, he comes smack into direct contact with Tradition Ten. It is his guarantee that his private life and beliefs are nobody else's business and that our Society protects these as sacred and crucial to AA unity.

All the same, being human, we now and then get a little off the

Traditions track. Occasionally a speaker will start to wax Christian, or vegetarian, or whole-earth-all-natural. Once the topic at a meeting was: "What can we do about the ozone layer, now that we're sober and globally aware?" Thank God there were enough experienced members in the room to get the meeting back to AA.

By neither backing nor attacking others either personally or in their beliefs, we are not likely to be attacked in return. By not endorsing or opposing anyone or anything, we are free to concentrate on the one thing we do best, which is to fix drunks. By not promoting schools of alcoholism theory or encouraging education through church groups or civic organizations, we stay out of alliances and out of the paper. The public doesn't get confused. And more important, we don't get confused.

Mindful of the "no public controversy" Tradition, I am supported in my personal recovery and all of us are supported two million strong and growing daily in service and recovery because we are united.

Jim N.
Denver, Colorado

# Spirit of Anonymity

January 2011
(From *Dear Grapevine*)

I waited for my copy of the October 2010 "Anonymity" issue, eager to hear how others were dealing with anonymity and the internet. I found good guidelines in the issue, but one problem I'm having was not addressed.

At various times, AA members have used my email address for religious chain letters, personal business promotions, and other non-AA related communication. I am on a service committee and gave my email address so that documents relating to our committee could be shared.

Recently, I opened an email from another committee member, and it was a rant against the president and his party. This was not only unsolicited, but inflammatory and insulting to me. I informed the sender that he'd violated our Tradition of having "no opinion on outside issues." He replied that he'd sent me the email as "one friend to another." I clarified that I'd not given him my email address as a friend, rather as a committee member.

It is true that the Traditions that guide us were written in a time and place so much different from today, but the spirit of anonymity is timeless and the wisdom to preserve it as available as ever.

Vickie A.
Oceanside, California

# None of My Business
October 2014

One day last October, as my turn to speak at my Traditions home group business meeting neared, I groaned as I realized I was about to talk about someone's car bumper stickers for yet a third or fourth year in a row. A sinking sensation came over me. What was wrong with me? Why couldn't I let this matter go?

I had noticed a car in the parking lot of our meeting recently with bumper stickers that I found very offensive. I was hoping I would never find out who the driver was, as I didn't want my view of their politics to affect what I thought of their recovery. Since AA has no opinion on outside issues, and individual AA members rarely express such opinions in meetings, I had come to the comfortable if not necessarily wise belief that if I liked a person's program, we most likely had the same political views.

This worked well enough for me, until one day I accidentally discovered whose car had the offensive stickers. It was a friend. By then, she'd added a second sticker that I also disagreed with. Then she added a third sticker that annoyed me! Meanwhile, here I was talking in my home group about how we have to practice the Tenth Tradition in the parking lots as well as the meeting rooms.

On a personal level my primary "tool" was to ignore the bumper stickers, but instead I found myself bringing it up again and again at our meetings. Ignoring wasn't working for me. So here's the tool I used …

I prayed for open-mindedness. Over time, I realized that I was the one with the problem. Because of my prayers, I've been freed from obsessing about the stickers, and I can now listen to this woman as I did of old. So far it's worked.

I even noticed recently that she's driving a different car, and I didn't even look to see what bumper stickers, if any, the new one is sporting.

B. L.

Madison, Wisconsin

## Opinions: Yours, Mine and Ours
October 1990

M ost of us understand the importance of Tradition Ten as it applies to AA as a whole. We have no trouble imagining what a fiasco would result if our General Service Office in New York began to endorse political candidates, support other causes, approve or disapprove of decisions made by religious bodies, or in any other way stray from our main objective.

It wouldn't be long before AA groups got into the act. There would be an AA-Alcoholics Back Big Bill for President Group in Biloxi, and an AA-Alcoholics Join John Jones Against Juveniles in Jail Group in Jacksonville. Eventually, I'm sure we'd wind up with an AA-Alcoholics Support International Nonsense In Nations Everywhere Group, which we could just call AA-ASININE for short. We can laugh about it only because it isn't happening, and that's because we have Tradition Ten.

But GSO in New York isn't the only representation we have. Our regional conferences, area assemblies, conventions and local central offices must also take care not to express themselves concerning any outside issues.

Individual members speaking to a nurses' association meeting, school, or business group, through an arrangement made by a public information committee, have the responsibility of not putting forth their own views as though they were those of AA, as does the speaker at an open meeting.

"The opinions you hear expressed here are those of the speakers and do not necessarily represent the opinion of AA as a whole." I hear that announcement, or one similar to it, at the beginning of many AA meetings. I'm embarrassed to admit how long I was a member of AA before, one night, it finally dawned on me: That's the Tenth Tradition!

Early in my sobriety I remember thinking, as I headed to a meeting, I wonder what my newfound friends will have to say about today's events. I can't remember what the events of that day were; maybe some political scandal that had broken or an election that had taken place. I know it was something of national importance, and I could hardly wait to hear what my fellow AA members thought about it.

The meeting started, a topic was introduced, and the discussion began. No one even mentioned the monumental event of the day. It might have been discussed over coffee later, but it wasn't a part of what was going on in that meeting room.

That's frequently the way AA meetings go, but not always. As individuals, we have lots of opinions, and we frequently express them in meetings. If you doubt this, the next time you're at your home group pretend there is someone with a bell who rings it every time an outside issue is mentioned. If that were to happen, that bell would soon be chiming so much that the meeting would sound like midnight in a clock factory.

Some of us talk about how our weird religious upbringing affected our thinking, or how angry we are about the latest decision of the city council. We may deride a corporation's stupid hiring practices, or mothers-in-law in general. But if some kind of disclaimer is read at the beginning of the meeting when we take off on one of these tangents, the visitor or newcomer doesn't think we are postulating a theory that belongs to AA.

What a gift the Tenth Tradition is to us in AA. It means that we don't have to bolt and run when someone—in a discussion meeting or from the podium—says something with which we don't agree. It allows us the privilege of "taking what we want and leaving the rest" from each member's comments.

Maybe even more important, it gives speakers an opportunity to say what they think. When our turn comes to speak, we are given the same incredible freedom of expression and it's understood that we speak as individuals, not for AA as a whole.

As much as I appreciate the right to express my opinion, I appreciate even more the wisdom of our early leaders in deciding that, as far as outside issues go, AA shouldn't have an opinion.

Fran D.
New Orleans, Louisiana

# Politically Incorrect
February 2005
(From *Dear Grapevine*)

'm writing with some urgency about the manifold violations of the Tenth Tradition in my neighborhood AA meetings—specifically, members of one political party venting anger about the candidate of an opposing party in meetings. Will supporters of the opposing party feel welcomed, accepted and safe with so many members voicing anger and even hatred of them and their views? And have those angry members thought about how they'd feel if the situation were reversed?

Grapevine is in a prime position to remind the more agitated members that our primary purpose is to stay sober and help other alcoholics, even if they have different political views. I hope you print my letter as a sober reminder on the Tenth Tradition: We have no opinion on outside issues such as religion and politics.

I've been sober 25 years in AA, North and South, and have never seen this kind of ostracizing behavior before. Let's not go the way of the Washingtonians!

Gail C.
New York, New York

## My Father, Myself
October 2008

Sometimes, I'm great at practicing the Tenth Tradition. Other times, I'm horrible at it. But my ability to apply this Tradition in my life has grown as I have gotten older in sobriety. I still slip up sometimes, as I think we all do. One guiding principle has become clear to me: I am practicing the spirit of the Tenth Tradition as long as I am sharing my experience, strength and hope, and not my opinions. By practicing this, I've been able to strengthen my relationships in and out of the rooms, including a difficult relationship with my father.

One of the sayings I've heard in the rooms for many years is, "We go to meetings to give, not to get." For me, the difference between being a "giver" and a "taker" is the quality of what I bring to meetings with me. Am I sharing my experience, strength and hope, or am I sharing my opinions? If I'm sharing my experience, strength and hope, I'm sharing about how the principles I've learned in AA—such as service, unity, reaching out for help, acceptance, faith or humility—have helped me to live life on life's terms just enough to stay sober for a few 24 hours. If I'm sharing my opinions, it sounds different, even to my ears. It sounds more like, "You should do this to stay sober," rather than, "This is what I did to stay sober."

In fact, sharing my opinions even feels different. It's almost as if I can feel that self-righteousness begin to seep out of my pores and coat me and whatever I say in an icky, prideful goo. This coating is usually preceded by my hearing something I disagree with in a meeting. Feeling my hand shoot up, I open my mouth to "correct" what I believe are my sober colleagues' delusions. Why I still feel sometimes, after years of sobriety, that it's my job to correct everyone's delusions is beyond me! Perhaps it's more manifestation of self-centered fear. Why else would I feel the need to always be right?

For many years, I would opine in meetings, saying things that were divisive, rude and hurtful, because I felt that I had the "right" brand of sobriety. Some people I directed my rants at 10 or more years ago still avoid me today. I can't say I blame them—it hurt when others did it to me. Talk about doing damage to group unity!

For me, the change in my thinking and sharing began when I had about five or six years of sobriety. An assignment from my sponsor meant I was to start practicing the Tenth Tradition with my family, specifically with my dad, as part of my amends toward him.

Basically, I had always felt afraid that I wasn't a good enough daughter for him, that he wished he'd had someone more normal, with fewer tattoos and fewer opinions that differed from his own. My fear that I wasn't good enough turned into a fear that he didn't love me. Being the kind of alcoholic I am and being a person from a loud, opinionated family, I decided that I'd alienate my dad by arguing with him about politics. That way, if he didn't seem to love me the way I wanted him to, I could chalk it up to politics—not to my deepest fears about our relationship.

Of course, that didn't work! In the course of an inventory, I realized that this was a ploy so that I didn't have to have a real relationship with my dad. I didn't want to risk finding out I wasn't what I thought he wanted me to be. I was used to arguing with my dad about politics, so that's what I did. Instead, I had to practice *not* arguing with him, one day at a time. This was hard—and scary. I actually had to talk to my dad about what was going on in my life, not about what was on the nightly news. It was much more personal. As time went on, it got easier. Still, there were a couple of times when I strayed, went into the personality of my politics, and ended up in shouting matches, complete with the sullen silences afterward.

As I learned how to have a real relationship with my dad, I learned that I could have a real relationship with other people based on this principle, too. When I talk about my opinions, I don't leave a lot of room to talk about my feelings, my hopes, my dreams, my aspirations, my life. I leave room for argument, but not for relating. That has been dangerous for me, both inside and outside AA. Arguments usually lead me right back to feelings of isolation, difference, anger and self-righteousness. These feelings, if left unchecked, could lead me back to a drink if I don't cut out the actions causing them.

I learned in AA of the principle of one alcoholic talking to another in the language of the heart. The logical extension of that principle is talking from the heart, one person to another. To me, this is something I feel I must aim for—it's part of practicing these principles in all of my affairs. And it allows me to be a giver in terms of my family, my job and my social affairs rather than to expect people in those areas of my life to kowtow to me.

Part of the reason this idea has become so important to me is that my dad, with whom I so struggled to be real, died about 10 years ago. Fortunately, I'd had about four or five years of practice relating to him, one person to another. I knew, when he died, that he loved me, even though we still occasionally butted heads. I had taken that leap of faith in AA and practiced talking with him, instead of arguing with him. I am not sure if either he or I would have believed in our love for each other had I avoided this work. By allowing me to have a relationship with him based on love and common ground, my nonalcoholic dad taught me something about AA: I need to have that relation with all of you, too.

Juliet H.
Pinole, California

# The Beauty of Tradition Ten
July 1991

Sobriety in AA is the first thing in my life that has really worked. I'm grateful to fellow AAs who've shown me how not to drink on a daily basis, and to alcoholics I've never met who established our Steps, Traditions and Concepts for World Service. When I live these principles to the best of my ability, they keep me sober and in touch with the God of my understanding.

I'm especially grateful for Tradition Ten, where it is suggested that AA groups never get involved in the messy business of debating outside issues. The wonderful "extra" implied by this Tradition is that I, as an individual recovering alcoholic, am free to simply enjoy sobriety in AA, without having to defend my position on any outside issue.

You see, I grew up in the sixties. I lived with my parents (one alcoholic, one social drinker) who were closely associated with a small, left-wing, private college in the Northeast. It was a school where expressing your opinions in public was very important. On campus, where I hung out as a 13-year-old, I heard lots of angry rhetoric about Vietnam, civil rights and a lot else. My parents brought the same kind of political anger home with them, and challenged me to come up with informed positions on the same issues. I was only an eighth grader, but I was expected to engage in adult-style discussions. If I didn't have an opinion on the issue at hand, I was considered a failure or a non-thinker.

Looking back, it was probably great training for a future alcoholic. I got very good at hiding the things I was truly ashamed of (especially the amount I drank), using a smoke screen of vaguely directed political opinion.

As my disease progressed, I was often broke, unemployed, hungover and in need of a place to stay. Usually, my parents would take me in, and for months at a time I'd live at home, trying to get my act together. Deep down inside I knew I was sick and crazy from booze. But at the time, dealing with it was too frightening. It was easier to engage my parents in a petty debate over some global issue beyond our control than to draw attention to the real reason I was out of work.

Today, I'm sober and grateful for what it was like, what happened, and what it's like now. I'm even grateful to my parents, who put up with me as an active alcoholic while also living with their own illnesses. But I'm especially grateful to the alcoholics who founded this Fellowship and gave us the guidelines by which we run our groups. Tradition Ten frees AAs to concentrate on what we have in common—recovery, unity, service—rather than waste time debating outside issues. Angry debate of things over which we have no power can only serve to split us.

Matt F.
Brooklyn, New York

# TRADITION ELEVEN

Our public relations policy is based on attraction
rather than promotion; we need always maintain personal
anonymity at the level of press, radio and films.

———————◆———————

*Providing an example of sobriety can be more powerful
than promoting AA.*

AA *is not a secret society—we carry the message wherever
we can. Information about alcoholism is constantly
being fed to the general public through "the colossus of
communication," as Bill W. notes, and AA members are doing what
they can to reach out to still suffering alcoholics around the globe.
Yet, in all this communication there is a line experience has taught
us we should not cross—the very fine line between attraction and
promotion.*

*"Much of the political, economic, and religious life of the world is
dependent upon publicized leadership," writes Bill W. "People who
symbolize causes and ideas fill a deep human need. We of AA do not
question that. But we do have to soberly face the fact that being in the
public eye is hazardous, especially for us." It is far better, Bill suggests,
to let our friends recommend us.*

*"To protect me, AA, and the suffering alcoholic, the message must be
carried anonymously," writes Sara G., author of the story, "The Message,
Not Me." "In carrying it 'unselfishly and well,' I become not 'me,'
but a 'power of example' ... I need to keep the 'me' out of the message."*

*"It reminds me that I never know who's watching," adds Lisa R. of
Aberdeen, South Dakota in "Put the Coffee On." "I need to be the best
example of the Big Book I can."*

# Why Should He Get All the Press Instead of Me?
November 2002

"Take a look at this; Joe broke his anonymity." I passed Sunday's Living Section across the table to my wife and pointed. "Right there."

A lead article in the state's most widely-circulated newspaper featured Alcoholics Anonymous and Al-Anon. "Joe" (not his real name) joined our home group just ahead of us but moved away. The good news was that he'd stayed sober since he left town. The bad news was that he identified himself as an alcoholic and said he'd joined a "Twelve Step Program of Recovery."

My wife read the offending paragraphs silently, while I picked up a copy of the Traditions and read out loud. "Our public relations policy is based on attraction rather than promotion; we need always maintain personal anonymity at the level of press, radio and films."

I slapped the magazine down on the table. "Notice, Joe didn't actually mention Alcoholics Anonymous. I suppose he squeaked through a loophole."

More halos than mine burned bright that day and well into the week as the meeting rooms filled with talk of "attraction versus promotion" and "cash register honesty." When people tired of Tradition Eleven as a topic, we started on Tradition Twelve, which says that "Anonymity is the spiritual foundation of all our traditions."

Most folks didn't pussyfoot around, either. They just gave Joe his lumps plain, albeit in absentia. I, on the other hand, demonstrated my advanced spiritual state and played by the "rules." I put "sharings" out on the tables all nicely gift-wrapped in "experience, strength and hope." Though if you'd pulled the pretty paper off the package I so generously offered, inside you'd have found the same figurative lump of coal—judgement and condemnation.

When I said out loud that maybe somebody ought to write the newspaper (I had me in mind, of course) and set them straight, an old-timer suggested, "You might want to read some of the early AA history and see how Bill W. struggled with this issue." So, I widened my horizons.

*Pass It On* helped me to flesh out my critique of Joe's breach of Tradition Eleven. Bill W. had prescribed anonymity as the antidote to "the dread neurotic germ of the power contagion." He himself had to take his own medicine for that contagion, too, when he turned down an honorary doctorate from Yale University.

This material lent my words of wisdom an almost scriptural weight. They might even, I thought, inspire poor, power-hungry Joe to repent and rejoin the fold in good standing.

But you know how it goes, don't you? It turned out the research I'd been doing wasn't for Joe. It was for me. Thankfully, my finely crafted words never went any further than the home group, because as I spoke them, Bill W.'s medicine worked, long-distance, on my own "power contagion." I experienced a sudden flash of insight: My problem with Joe was simple. Why should he get all the press, instead of me?

Was it my imagination, or did the old-timer who pushed me toward *Pass It On* laugh heartiest of all when I shared that revelation? Then again, maybe he laughed heartiest because he knew the lesson still wasn't over the day I claimed that insight as uniquely mine. Mercifully, he left it to me to re-discover what I'd heard said so often: If it's got a name, it's been done.

As I put these memories down on paper 10 years later, I re-opened *Pass It On* to remind myself of what I'd read and got a mild shock as I read these words, as if for the first time: "Bill's own response to Rollie's 'transgression' was to seek out publicity for himself."

One of the nicest things about AA is the company we keep (even when we don't know it)!

Don P.
St. Albans, Vermont

# Put the Coffee On

November 2008

It was Wednesday again, and I was late for work, as usual. I flipped through the mail, stacks of unpaid bills. I never seemed to be able to pay them. I made a decent living managing a restaurant—I'd simply concluded that I was a terrible money manager. It cost me many sleepless nights.

I loved my job. Most of my life I had been painfully shy, introverted, or just too darn selfish to meet and get to know people. I was 17 years old and scared most of the time. Every day at my restaurant, though, I got to be an actress. As I stepped over the threshold into the restaurant, I became a star on stage. I honestly felt that way. I forgot about being shy and performed. I made jokes, smiled a lot and kidded the regulars. I had a ball.

And I looked forward to Wednesdays. Wednesdays were good days because it was busy. My favorite group came in every Wednesday at about 9:20 P.M. They congregated in the back room, pushing tables together and laying out ashtrays. We would then start the coffee rolling, and man, could they drink! They were polite to all my staff, even if we messed up an order.

What interested me the most was the laughter. It was real belly laughing, the kind that makes you smile even if you didn't hear the joke. My office was just adjacent to the back room. Sometimes I would hold a glass up to the wall to hear what they were laughing about. I would be sad, because they laughed about things I sometimes cried about. I found myself pouring coffee back there probably more often than necessary. Occasionally I would have coffee with them. They stayed until about 11 P.M. or so, then they congregated in the parking lot for the "good-bye scene."

Eventually, I started to plan special things for Wednesday nights. I might bake a cake just for them. One time, I put colorable place mats down, and they actually colored them. The next week I had the place mats hanging from the ceiling. They laughed so hard! Once, I was heading to my car to go home, and they were still in the parking lot. I stopped to say good-bye and found myself shaking hands with each of them. This became routine. They all knew me by name, and I was starting to learn theirs.

One night, one of them, Kevin, handed me a card. It had the name of a church followed by "Aberdeen Wednesday Night AA Group." He said, "Maybe you would like to come and see why we are so goofy!" I had no idea my life was about to change dramatically.

The next Wednesday night before work I went to one of their open meetings. I knew everyone there, but it felt different than it did in my restaurant. My stage was gone.

Someone shared from the podium what it used to be like, what happened and what it was like now. I fought away tears. When they talked about what it used to be like, they talked about feelings I felt every day: inadequacy, inferiority, and overwhelming loneliness. I had never really thought of my drinking as a problem; it had always seemed like the answer. Sometimes it would take away the nervous edge I felt in groups of people. Sometimes drinking would help me sleep at night, when the voices in my head wouldn't be quiet. Sometimes it made the guilt and shame I felt diminish a little. After that first meeting, I started to wonder if drinking might be a problem for me. I went to a few more open meetings. I curbed my drinking for several months. I thought I couldn't go to their meetings if I was drinking.

June 3, 1983, was my 18th birthday. I'd planned the night carefully to avoid drinking. I went out to eat with older friends. It went really well—so well that I thought I could have a little white wine after dinner. Then came the vodka, then the beer, then the Amarillo slammers, and the next thing I knew, I woke up late for work. Work was a disaster. The cook didn't show, waitresses were disorganized, I was suffering from a major hangover. Then my "friends" started to show up to recite what I had done the night before. I had really tried not to drink.

Now I was afraid I couldn't not drink. Everything I heard the AAs talk about at meetings came flooding back.

The next Wednesday, I went to a closed meeting.

Fast forward 20 years: Here I sit thinking about attraction rather than promotion and personal anonymity at the level of press, radio and films. My whole story is based on attraction. I didn't even know they were from AA; I was just attracted to them. It reminds me that I never know who is watching. I need to be the best example of the Big Book I can, all the time.

Now, about personal anonymity. I am forever grateful "those guys" weren't afraid to let me know they went to AA. I may never have gotten here. I am not a manager at that restaurant anymore. I went to college, graduated, and work in my field. I have worked at the same place for 16 years. I have a husband (I spilled water on him one of those Wednesday nights). We have two children and a granddaughter. I am happy and comfortable. I have had the benefit of active sponsorship and have been involved in all aspects of service work in AA. I have a home group and friends I love dearly. I have a deep and meaningful relationship with God. To think, I just came to see why they acted goofy!

Lisa R.
Aberdeen, South Dakota

# The Price of a Postage Stamp
November 2008
(From *Dear Grapevine*)

Around 1977, I wrote to Grapevine to get support for a postal stamp celebrating the 50th anniversary of AA. I had received support and letters of recommendation to the postal department from congressmen, senators, and alcoholism counselors' professional organizations.

I was disappointed to get a response referencing this Tradition and denial of placing an article in Grapevine encouraging members to write letters of support. No stamp was ever issued featuring AA. Time passed and I gained a better understanding of the intention behind our Traditions and the wisdom in Grapevine's decision.

The Traditions are for our unity, but, like the Steps, they also benefit personal recovery. Being self-supporting, having an ultimate authority (a loving God), staying out of public controversy—just to name a few—have benefited my recovery and serenity. It was my attraction to the AA lifestyle that kept me coming back long enough to find sobriety and continue to celebrate recovery.

Ronald S.
Prescott Valley, Arizona

## Self-Promotion, Not Attraction
November 2006

On the last Thursday of each month, our Alcoholics Anonymous meeting covers one of the Traditions. Frequently, the Tradition Eleven meeting falls on Thanksgiving, and we conveniently change it into a gratitude meeting.

After all, how does the question of breaking one's anonymity in public affect most of us non-celebrities? That's the terrain of rock stars and golfers who blab in public about how they went to rehab, joined "the program," and are now sober. Then we read a news story about the car they drove into a telephone pole and their return to some exclusive recovery center in the Bahamas.

During my first failed tour of duty in AA in 1980, I learned just how easy it is for a regular civilian to break Tradition Eleven and do real damage to our treasured Fellowship. My lovely young wife had given up on me after a year of marriage. The husband-to-be she had met a year-and-a-half earlier didn't drink, although he smoked some dope.

He certainly wasn't the reeling, retching, obnoxious animal she lived with now. "Either the booze goes, or I go," she said. It was a mandate; I decided to give AA a try.

After attending meetings for about a month, I had things pretty well figured out. I attended one meeting a week and showed up late. That way, I never had to say, "Hi, I'm Michael and I'm an alcoholic." I never shared and left early to avoid any chitchat with the riffraff who frequented the meetings.

However, I decided I would read the literature, study real hard, and learn how not to drink. If I did my assignments, I would pass the course with flying colors.

Months passed and things got better. Married life improved and things at work took a decided upswing. When my coworkers asked what the change was due to, I said—with pride—that I was in AA. Spouting chapter and verse, I impressed my colleagues. I came to be known as Mr. AA and did a good job of lording my superior knowledge over the others. I told my former drinking buddies that they could probably use some of what I had. After all, look at how my life had turned around. A few of them seriously considered it.

But working the Steps, getting a sponsor, practicing real honesty, acceptance and faith in a Higher Power just wasn't part of my program. I didn't need that stuff; I could do it my way. We all know what happened.

First, I convinced my wife that I could drink wine on the weekends. Because she came from a good alcoholic family, that made sense to her. When that didn't get too far out of control, we agreed I could drink a little wine during the week. Then, some hard stuff on the weekends and, within a few months, I was back to a quart of vodka a day.

My coworkers noticed. It wasn't just that I was drinking again. I showed up for work late, had the shakes, memory loss, and erratic mood swings, and was frequently ill. I made a foolish spectacle of myself and they let me know it. "Well, Mr. AA, what happened to you?" they asked. "I thought you AAs weren't allowed to drink? I guess that AA program isn't so good after all."

That is how I broke Tradition Eleven. I misinformed many people about AA and how it really works. My poor performance may have provided a great excuse to any number of people who could have benefited from our program. Although I did a great disservice to the Fellowship, I learned my lesson.

In 1990, I crawled back into the rooms. I was in a lot more pain than I had been a decade earlier. This time around, I arrived on time, spoke up, got a sponsor, participated and took suggestions. Today, I keep my mouth shut unless an opportunity to help another alcoholic presents itself. Because the program saved my life, I treasure all that it has to offer me.

I may not have the opportunity to speak to the multitudes about my participation in AA, but I can abuse Tradition Eleven just as surely as if I were front and center on the latest, hottest, television reality show.

Michael F.
Millington, New Jersey

# The Message, Not Me
November 1992

"No! Not me!" was my instant reaction to hearing the message on my phone machine from our local intergroup. A writer for a national women's magazine was looking for AA women to interview—if I wanted to talk with her, here was the number to call. I just automatically decided to refuse because I'd gotten so sick of what has become the "recovery industry" and the media attention to it; of the silly, inaccurate articles and self-serving books; and of the big and not-so-big shots who broke their anonymity consistently at very public levels.

True, "No! Not me!" was (and often is) my reaction to much about my experience in Alcoholics Anonymous—to much about my alcoholism itself. I wasn't an alcoholic (never mind that both of my parents were, that I'd been having blackouts for years, etc.); I could control my drinking, with just a little more willpower (except that I couldn't). I didn't need AA! Until I did.

I knew about AA because I wrote books and articles that dealt with it. I knew it worked—it had worked for my father. But a lot of it didn't apply to me. I wasn't crazy or sick; I had my teeth and a place to live; I had always taken good care of myself. I understood, of course, that there were a lot of things you needed. You needed to keep it simple, to take it easy, to work your way slowly through recovery. I could manage my life quite well, thank you. All I had was this drinking problem that had gotten out of control. I knew that AA could help me stop drinking (though I had no idea how)—and that was all I wanted.

I gave no thought to wanting to be happy: that was OK for you, too. Maybe I didn't even know I was unhappy, but I was—miserable, in fact. In agony.

And though I was happy not to be drinking any more, I wasn't happy with a lot about AA. The Steps I would follow well enough to pass your tests. The Traditions made little sense, but I could see that they were important to you, so I would be polite about them. As for your "literature" and publicity materials—well, to be polite, they didn't ring any bells for me.

Then something did ring a bell loud enough to awaken me to the fact that AA meant something more to me than a self-improvement project. This was hearing someone explain: The Steps were there to protect me from booze; the Traditions were there to protect AA from me. That rang bells because I'm the type of drunk who, from her first meeting, knew some better ways for AA to operate. Take those publications—I already had plans to improve them. After all, that was my profession, right? You were lucky to have my skills available. (The fact that what brought me to AA was the imminent loss of that profession escaped me temporarily.)

So you see that by the time the years had rolled around to the moment when I heard that phone message, "No, not me!" was actually a sign of progress. Because, fortunately for me and for AA, I had settled into a Traditions-minded home group with a Traditions-conscious, service-oriented sponsor. And when after a few years I became a GSR and read (in one of those "inadequate" pamphlets) that I was a "guardian of the Traditions," I really took them seriously, and decided that perhaps I didn't have to fix something that obviously wasn't broken.

Before the twelve-step recovery programs of all sorts became big business and hot news a while back, though, I was of two minds about AA publicity. On the one hand I don't know if I would have found my way to my first AA meeting if the folks who pushed my dad into the program hadn't read about it in the press, or if famous people hadn't made public testimonials.

Sure, I could understand that anonymity was the foundation of the program—that's what helped people feel safe enough to come in. Easy to see that. (The "spiritual foundation" only began to make sense much later.) But this kind of press attention was such a good draw! Public relations is one of the ways I've pieced together a living, and in PR, one wants to promote. If possible, one does that subtly, by making it look like "attraction"—by, for instance, putting a testimonial for one's product or service in the mouth of somebody famous. It's the opposite of anonymity.

On the other hand, as time went on, I realized that these celebrities didn't only get sober—they sometimes got drunk. That's what PR people call bad press. Not only that, but as I got more sophisticated in sobriety, it began to occur to me that there might even be a connection between their public anonymity breaks and their subsequent slips. After all, I know my own reaction to getting praise from outsiders for my "strength" and "willpower" in staying sober. What an invitation to grandiosity! One might almost feel cured.

And when other writers have—in my view—begun using their sobriety to get best-sellers, I've been startled by my rage. Only part of that righteous indignation derived from envy; the rest, I honestly feel, was a sign of progress as to how precious had become the program and its principles. Challenge tradition? Not me.

Whatever the sources of my motives, of course I shouldn't talk to that reporter! Not me. Or should I? Think think think (those slogans apply to me now, too). In another sign of progress, I didn't just act on my initial urge. Instead, I did some other things I've learned to do (often despite myself): I talked to my sponsor and others with experience to share—and listened to what they had to say. At their suggestion I read about the Eleventh Tradition.

Bill wrote that "100 percent personal anonymity before the public is just as vital to the life of AA as 100 percent sobriety is to the life of each and every member." Serious stuff. He also wrote that "nothing can matter more to the future welfare of AA than the manner in which we use this colossus of communication. Used unselfishly and well, the results can surpass our present imagination." Unselfishly and well: could I do that?

When all else fails, read the instructions. Tradition Eleven itself says, "Our public relations policy is based on attraction rather than promotion; we need always maintain personal anonymity at the level of press, radio and films."

There are two parts there, and it seems to me they add up to more than the whole. To "attract," the message must be carried. To protect me, AA and the suffering alcoholic, the message must be carried anonymously. In carrying it "unselfishly and well," I become not "me," but a "power of example." I can not only spread the word about the program and about anonymity, but I can also demonstrate the principle of anonymity by practicing it. I need to keep the "me" out of the message.

Who, me? Yes, me. I could—and I probably should, especially because of what I do in my life "outside" AA, which has provided regular experience in both interviewing and being interviewed. Is that being what Bill called a "power-driver"? Not if I follow the guidelines of the Tradition and just say no if the writer presses beyond its boundaries. "Anonymity is humility at work," Bill wrote.

Besides, if I didn't talk with this reporter, I could never again justifiably complain about the poor quality of press coverage of AA!

So I called, and I'm glad I did, because the interview was a success:

not a success as in big-shotism, but an AA-style success. I kept my anonymity, for one thing. The writer seemed to completely understand this Tradition, and respected it. She didn't even ask me what I did for a living, and she asked me how—and if—I'd like to be identified. (I also had a chance to practice my humility by not suggesting better ways for her to conduct her interview!) I was able to help one of what Bill called "our friends in the press" to tell our story for us and to clear up some aspects of it which she didn't understand and which (because of what I had learned from my group, my sponsor, and my service experience) I was able to explain.

It also seemed that in researching "women in AA," her focus was more on "women" than on "AA," more on feminist issues, self-improvement, and relationships than on freedom from the agony of alcoholism. As a woman in AA, I could tell her that what's important about the program is that it keeps me sober. The rest—be it personal growth or personal pronouns removed from their historical context—is conversation.

And how did her article on "women in AA" turn out? OK, I guess—but that's really none of my business. And because I kept "my business" out of it, it was a success in terms of AA and the Traditions. It was also a success for me because, like every other kind of AA service, it brought an unsought gift.

In the midst of some miscellaneous questions, the reporter suddenly asked, "Are you happy?" And I, just as suddenly, answered, "Yes." I surprised myself because, you see, I'm the kind of glass-half-empty drunk who'll tell you everything that's wrong with my health, love life, work, finances—and forget the important part: I'm sober. Just as, in the beginning (and sometimes today), I'd tell you everything that's wrong with the program and the people in it and take for granted the most important fact: It works. The rest is, indeed, conversation.

When the interview ended, the reporter thanked me. "Thank you," I responded, as my sponsor had explained early on was the appropriate thing to say to anyone who had allowed me to perform a service.

For it was a service, to AA, and to me. And alone in my kitchen, I felt the flow of what Bill called "the spiritual energy that moves us along the road to full liberation." Energy, yes; freedom, yes. And with it—happiness. Yes, me.

Sara G.
New York, New York

# Don't Be a Stranger
December 2009

"Could you get a card for Bob S.? He's in the hospital and not doing well," a person asked at a recent meeting. I knew quite a few Bob S.'s and I wondered if he was one of them. After the meeting, I looked for the person who'd asked about the card, but he'd already left. I felt as though a chance to be helpful may have gone with him.

For me, anonymity within the Fellowship insures a reduction in my ability to be useful. It's interesting that Dr. Bob is credited with the belief that there are two ways to break one's anonymity. The obvious one is to be identified by name or photo at the level of press, radio and film. The other was not to use full names at meetings of Alcoholics Anonymous.

In my Cooperation with the Professional Community and Public Information work outside of AA meetings, I diligently protect the anonymity of myself and other AAs. Press, radio, film, television and new technologies such as the internet certainly require our complete anonymity. I believe that's the intention of Tradition Eleven.

Introducing ourselves at AA functions isn't mentioned. When I introduce myself, ask for a card, or converse with other members of the Fellowship, I make it clear who I am and about whom I am speaking. In that way, we all know the who, and how we can be of service.

Rick B.
Gahanna, Ohio

# Mike the Plumber and Airplane Tim?
November 2014

I was prompted to write this after visiting a meeting in south Florida with my wife. While talking to some people before it started, someone mentioned "Emphysema Mike." My wife almost burst out laughing. Everywhere I've lived and traveled since getting sober in 1990, people in AA have had nicknames. But never had she heard someone identified by a malady.

In my home group we have such characters as Mike the Plumber, Airplane Tim, the Good Dave (self-proclaimed) and so forth. While these monikers are descriptive and sometimes amusing, I believe they do us a disservice. Besides sounding a little like an organized crime family, more importantly they highlight the fact that we might be taking the principle of anonymity beyond its original intention.

My sponsor has introduced himself at meetings by his first and last names since I've known him. One day he told me I should do the same. By way of explanation, he had me read several passages from the book *Dr. Bob and the Good Oldtimers*. John, my sponsor, said we are not anonymous among ourselves. What if for some reason I have to look up your phone number or come visit you in the hospital? I think they may have a hard time finding Airplane Tim. Dr. Bob said we had taken this business of anonymity way too far.

In *Dr. Bob and the Good Oldtimers* there are several comments by Dr. Bob, or people recalling what he said regarding anonymity. My favorite is a recollection by Warren C. of the doctor saying, "... there were two ways to break the anonymity Tradition: 1) by giving your name at the public level of press or radio; 2) by being so anonymous that you can't be reached by other drunks."

The next segment contains another quote attributed to Dr. Bob about the Eleventh Tradition: "Since our Tradition on anonymity designates the exact level where the line should be held, it must be obvious to everyone who can read and understand the English language that to maintain anonymity at any other level is definitely a violation of this Tradition." Several more quotes follow using equally adamant language in the next several paragraphs.

If my sponsor tells me to do something, I assume it's with good reason. When he goes out of his way to tell me where to find out why he told me to do it, I'm compelled to seek out his explanation. After having read the above quotes and discussing them with my sponsor and other members about eight years ago, I now always identify myself at meetings by my full name, as do several members of my home group and the men I sponsor. While I know there are no Traditions police, I try to do what I can today to help people who want to know our founders' intent when they wrote Tradition Eleven.

Jim T.

Longmont, Colorado

# TRADITION TWELVE

Anonymity is the spiritual foundation of all our traditions, ever reminding us to place principles before personalities.

———————◆———————

*Sacrifice is the watchword of anonymity.*

"At my first meeting I was full of fear and ashamed of being an alcoholic," writes the author of the article, "Scared to Be Seen"— a state in which many of us have found ourselves, as well.

Often in these moments, a hand reaches out—the hand of AA. "Somebody ... buttonholed me before I had time to sneak out," he writes. "He told me not to worry, that AA would protect my anonymity."

Similarly, Bernice M. in the story, "Our Protective Mantle," writes "Even now the people who come to us for help are ashamed, afraid, asking the same old questions: How could this have happened to me? What must other people think of me?

"We invite those newcomers to crawl under the warm tent of anonymity with us," she continues, "where they can be seen only by the eyes of those who have felt the same incomprehensible demoralization that they are feeling. We don't even ask their names.

"With all your secrets safely shrouded in anonymity, we get to know who you really are ... get acquainted with what, for lack of a better word, I'll call your soul.

"There are only two words in the name of this Fellowship to which we belong. The second word, 'anonymous,' defines us ... It is part of what gets and keeps us well."

It is, in fact, our foundation.

# Scared to Be Seen
December 2013

At my first meeting I was full of fear and ashamed of being an alcoholic. I would have surrendered several years earlier had it not been for my inflated ego that kept me from accepting the fact that I could no longer drink like a normal person. Alcohol, which had been my friend for the first 10 years of my drinking career, turned into a dangerous enemy during my last five.

Paradoxically, in spite of my low self-esteem, my sick inflated ego tried to tell me at that first meeting that I was somebody special and therefore should look for more appropriate help elsewhere, rather than from a "leper colony." What if someone spotted me and advised my four remaining clients that their consultant was an alcoholic and not to be trusted? Furthermore, had I during my first weeks in AA heard participants in open AA meetings use last names, I would have used it as an excuse to run away from AA because to stay might lead to my anonymity being broken to the wrong persons.

Somebody at my first meeting, who looked vaguely familiar, buttonholed me before I had time to sneak out. This man, Dennis, had apparently seen me visiting his company and noticed that I looked like I had an alcohol problem. He told me not to worry, that AA would protect my anonymity, and that the members of this group—an open meeting—were mostly white-collar workers who, because of their jobs and status in their community, had to keep their affiliation with AA a well-guarded secret. He informed me that at AA meetings people were told not to break anyone's anonymity, not even their own. The use of full names could be dangerous for professionals and definitely scare some newcomers away.

At the time I did not know that only a small percentage of first-time visitors actually stay in AA long enough to qualify for their first milestone: a three-month chip. Therefore, hearing full names could send publicity-shy persons back to continue their descent toward alcoholic unhappiness and death. Bill W. in his last message stated that, "The principle of anonymity must remain our primary and enduring safeguard."

Thanks to Dennis, I joined that group, found a sponsor and got support from his cronies. In the beginning, I needed and received a lot of stroking and positive reinforcement. Eventually, I understood that they did this to teach me that helping other alcoholics would help me to stay sober. My sponsor encouraged me to do service work, but warned me of the temptation to hide behind job titles to avoid working the program. He also pointed out that rigorous honesty with myself, the Steps, and helping others would eventually replace my inflated ego with humility, turn my low self-esteem into self-respect, and lead me to a happy and joyous life.

Some are sicker than others. Early on it was suggested that I seek psychiatric help. So I did. Luckily for me, I found someone who knew our Twelve Step program. He could read me like an open book. He even shocked me by pointing out that my choice of attention-getting neckties made me no different from other newcomers with odd-looking haircuts and bizarre clothes. According to him, such individuals had grown up in varying versions of loveless and dysfunctional homes. Prior to coming to AA we escaped into alcohol to dull our feelings of inadequacy and low self-esteem. This left a deep hole that craved to be filled with attention and stroking.

A third of a century ago I was told, "It will get better"—and it has. My wife of 24 years and I recently took our cakes together, celebrating 71 years of combined sobriety. Thanks to Alcoholics Anonymous, we live a happy and harmonious life one day at a time. And thank you Dennis, for making me feel safe when I first got here.

Anonymous

# Just Another Drunk
August 1981

Tradition Twelve never meant much to me until I left the security and non-anonymity of my home group. By "non-anonymity," I mean that my home group knew me, all of me; I had nothing hidden from them.

They had taken me in, a nonperson drunk in the final stages of alcoholism and all the despair that goes with it. They had patiently, and sometimes not so patiently, listened to my eternal poor mes and why mes. All I asked for when I first got to AA was pity. I didn't know enough or have sense enough to ask for sobriety. I didn't even have "the only requirement for membership."

They didn't give me pity—they gave me love. They ignored my symptoms and treated my disease by telling me, no matter what I said was wrong with me, "Don't drink, and go to meetings." And in meeting after meeting of sharing their experiences, they taught me slowly, one meeting at a time, how to begin to take one Step at a time, and they came to know me thoroughly.

My home group, a beloved family, watched me grow and get well. My sponsor watched me become a sponsor. I felt their love and pride in me and their joy in my growth in AA sobriety. I felt it and knew it because I, in turn, experienced those feelings with newer members. It was a happy time, and my open and honest sharing in my home group made me well-known and oh, so very comfortable.

Jobs and responsibilities were given to me as I became more capable. Eventually, I was able to do a few worthwhile projects to help the still-suffering alcoholic. I felt sober and successful, and this very peak experience led me to come out West where a new job awaited.

For over a year now, in several states, I have begun anew with several AA groups and many members. I've gotten a glimpse of that idea of anonymity as a spiritual foundation. Somehow, living alone in each new and strange place and going unknown to a meeting, I was really just another drunk. It was a humbling and good way to start all over. I listened to the same wonderful words coming from the mouths of strangers, and I knew that only their faces were unknown to me.

This understanding of them—a spiritual understanding and a knowing of them because of the AA program—gave me a glimpse of the meaning of the Twelfth Tradition. It was a hint of the meaning of humility, and I found it satisfying. I think it became satisfying because I now had to use the tools I'd been given. I needed to live the slogans and the Steps. I read the Big Book with care. I read copies of Grapevine that had been carefully selected back home and brought along. Those pages are just like meetings, and in a town where I had no phone numbers to give comfort between meetings or at odd hours, they played a vital role in keeping me sober and comfortable.

I found I became intensely aware of two spiritual ideas: Myself as a "personality" with a chance to grow, because I was truly anonymous in each new group; and the AA "principles" I had to turn to, because I did not have my known and loved home group to fall back on. I was on my own, alone and unknown, and at the same time not alone. An AA miracle!

At those first few (and I do mean few) meetings when my travels began, I was just another drunk, trying to stay sober. No one knew how wonderful I might be, nor how sick and rotten I might be either. But the love was there and was given to me. Somehow, it was very powerful. I was amazed to find myself accepting it humbly and with an awareness of the goodness of anonymity.

After those first meetings, I shared my story and myself, and so I then belonged to each new group. Though I was no longer anonymous to those fellow members, I had gained a precious bit of learning about anonymity as a "spiritual foundation."

A. M.
Santa Cruz, California

# Making Myself Anonymous
December 2008

T radition Twelve seems like a Step to me. It's so spiritual in its focus on anonymity. Someone said it well: "What is shared in meetings is more important than who said it."

The hard part for me is to remember that I, too, am a personality. When I start thinking that what I share is really important, that people really need to hear me ... well, I've put my own personality before the very principles I am attempting to convey. I start to think of myself as being uniquely capable of transmitting the message of recovery from alcoholism. Suddenly, I am the person everyone needs to hear!

Sure. How boring. Yet, predictable. As a lifelong know-it-all, people-pleaser, caretaker, mind-reader, problem-fixer, and control freak, I am incredibly susceptible to believing my own propaganda. Of course, pretty soon someone lets me know that I am really very dispensable, and my input or advice isn't needed, thank you very much. When I go to meetings, I am reminded that I am one among many. This is truly a "we" program.

Other people's recovery doesn't depend solely on me. There are so many terrific people in the program who can help other alcoholics, including me.

Julie E.
Maplewood, New Jersey

# Saved by the Bell
December 2014

I had my last drink on March 26, 1972. I had no problem with a Higher Power. Just looking up into the heavens at night convinced me that something a lot larger than mankind was at work. Though life had improved dramatically after I stopped drinking, the first few years were difficult employment-wise. I had a couple of dead-end jobs, and by my fourth AA birthday I was still scuffling. It appeared that in my line of work (sales) most companies were reluctant to hire someone like me: single, in my 40s, with some blank spaces on my resumé. In discussions with older members, I got suggestions that I didn't need to be completely honest about my AA affiliation when applying for work. However I wanted to be completely honest, and usually told my would-be employer that I was a member of AA. In some cases it didn't seem to matter, but some prospective employers who obviously knew nothing about AA seemed horrified at the thought of an alcoholic working for them.

In an effort to improve my resumé and employment prospects, I was taking evening courses in business administration at our local community college. When one of my classmates found out that I was looking for work he suggested I apply for a job with the company where he worked. He explained that the job would be advertised in our local paper, and that I seemed to have the credentials his company was looking for. It looked like a wonderful opportunity.

I carefully scrutinized the employment wanted ads and sure enough, in a couple of weeks the job was posted. I sent in an application and, after some preliminary back and forth discussion, was asked to come in for an interview. This was to take place at 2:30 P.M. The two gentlemen for whom I'd be working interviewed me. They had a tall stack of resumés on their desk; they had been interviewing all day and looked tired. This, they told me, was the last interview for the day. They seemed to approve of my qualifications; one of them had a similar background to mine, including business administration at the same community college I was attending.

After going over all the key points, I was asked, "Do you belong to any clubs or organizations?" Just as I was about to tell them I was a member of AA, there was a loud "Ding! Ding!" in the hallway. One of the men said, "It's the coffee wagon. Would you like a cup?" To which I replied, "Sure." After we drank our coffees the interview was over and their question about clubs or organizations was forgotten.

I left the meeting feeling good about my chances of getting the job. Later, after all the candidates were interviewed, I was asked to come in for another interview. This one would probably determine if the job was mine. Once again the interview took place in mid-afternoon, and again my interview was the last of the day. As in the prior interview, things went well and the men seemed satisfied with my credentials. After we had discussed all the relevant points, I was again asked, "Do you belong to any clubs or organizations?" Being a slow learner I was about to tell them of my AA membership, but before I could get a word out, once again we heard a "Ding! Ding!" The men asked me if I'd like a cup of coffee, and I accepted. We drank our coffees, and, amazingly, the subject of clubs or organizations never came up again.

I got a job that turned out to be very rewarding (from which I'm now retired), thanks to the intervention of the coffee wagon. The chances that it was a coincidence that the coffee wagon saved me—not once but twice—is a prospect too remote to contemplate. I'm thoroughly convinced that someone upstairs was telling me to "Shut up." I know that if the coffee wagon had not arrived when it did, I probably wouldn't have gotten that wonderful job.

Ron B.
Winnipeg, Manitoba

# Coping with Cliques

May 1974

(From *Dear Grapevine*)

Ever since I became a member of AA, many 24-hours ago, one criticism has been repeated and repeated. Perhaps our groups should pay more attention to it. I would like to tell you what one member has done about it.

The Twelfth Tradition suggests that we put principles above personalities. When I came to AA, I found that, particularly among the women, there were cliques. If you were a single gal, you were not invited to homes for even a cup of coffee. When you needed a ride, you got it—but only to and from the meeting.

I began to become resentful. Then I started to stay away from meetings. But I shortly realized that I was only hurting myself, and I accepted the situation as it was and tried to find ways of coping. I went to meetings for me and my sobriety. I listened and participated. I called members when I felt I needed advice or conversation. I picked up newcomers and people needing rides.

There are still cliques, but they no longer cause me hurt or ill feelings. In fact, I don't notice them. AA principles have given me a new, richer, fuller life, which I would not have known if I had not practiced principles above personalities.

M. C. S.
Santa Rosa, California

# Principles Before My Personality
December 1997

"My best thinking got me where I was." How many times, I wonder, have I heard that? Being a 24-year-old, less-than-two-years-sober college student, every time I heard it was too many. However, this AA pseudo-slogan has led me to become very skeptical of my own "best thinking." Today I must think about things in depth and discuss them with someone else—usually, though not exclusively, with one of my sponsors—before I can act with any degree of confidence. One of the greatest gifts AA has given me is the ability to think before I act. This was no door prize, mind you. I had to work very hard to earn this gift (though unfortunately, I don't always use it).

When I thought of the Twelfth Tradition, if I thought of it at all, I usually concentrated on the word "personalities." I mainly thought of other people's personalities and how I should practice the principles of AA as I saw them—sharing, caring, listening, accepting, and being honest, open and willing—regardless of whether or not I was kindly or pleasantly disposed toward other people's personalities. I would sometimes, in difficult or uncomfortable situations with a fellow AA, remind myself that I needn't like people to accept them; I should give them the same respect and courtesy that I would want. I should be willing to overlook any personality conflicts I might have with an individual and work the Steps of this wonderful program—unbiased.

However, as I continued to add days to the sum of my sobriety, I found it increasingly difficult to put principles before personalities. I was having all sorts of conflicts with people. It became apparent that this was going to be one of those things I could not afford to ignore much longer.

I began by seeking one of my sponsor's counsel. (When all else fails, I follow the instructions.) He told me that the only way to successfully deal with a problem is to confront it, to own it, and to change it. He has been sober over 18 years, so I thought I had best take his word on this. These ideas were not at all attractive to me, but I had two choices: deal with the problem and grow, or continue to suppress the problem and possibly drink as a result. I chose to deal with it.

What this ultimately involved was sitting in meeting rooms and openly admitting that I was having trouble accepting the rest of the alcoholics in the group. I was afraid to look into anyone else's eyes so I spoke only to the chairpeople. I said that I felt I was losing my ability to communicate, that I could not talk to another alcoholic—anyone for that matter—without conflict arising. I told the group, "I always have the best of intentions. I never want to hurt or hinder anyone. I want to help people. Whenever I talk to other people in this program, I only want to make them feel better. I want to make someone laugh or smile, be happy. Yet, more and more, the very people I am trying to help tell me to get off my high horse, stop lecturing, lighten up, and stop being so arrogant! I really don't understand what I'm doing wrong."

Right about then, a little 15-watt lightbulb went off over my head. What was happening was really pretty simple. It was as if when sharing, in the group or one-on-one with my sponsors or sponsees, I was unable to convey my true feelings and meanings. They seemed to be getting lost or distorted between their places of origin and their destinations. The fact was, I was not practicing and placing the principles before my personality. Every time I got ready to share something I was polishing and packaging what I would say to sound as good and grammatically correct, as spiritually on target, as possible.

Now I could see why people said I sounded like some lecturing college professor. I could see why they saw me as conceited. "So that's why they all think I'm a smart aleck!" I said with a great sigh of relief. My pride was injured, of course, but at least now I could see what I was doing wrong and what I needed to do to change it. I needed to apply the spiritual principle of anonymity to me when I tried to help and share. This personal facet of the Twelfth Tradition is the one I must practice daily to stay in recovery. In working the AA program, I need to be a recovering alcoholic first and an individual, with a personality, second.

Mark C.
Laurel, Mississippi

## Anonymity and Me
February 1975

I had been sober four months. I had kept my AA membership a dark secret. The inevitable day arrived when I received an invitation to my Uncle Paddy's home for one of our frequent liquid family celebrations. Everyone greeted me with hoots of approval, telling me how marvelous I looked. I walked through the clan gathering all evening drinking soda. My hand trembled each time I poured a soft drink. After five hours, my Aunt Sarah looked at me and said, "I see you are drinking it in soda now, Ed." I was amazed. They had not paid the least attention to what I had poured in my glass!

I made the decision to "break an AA Tradition." I told them my secret. They all agreed as how it was a grand thing and they were all meaning to mention my drinking to me one of these days and they knew that AA was not full of bums anyway. The trauma of that evening could have been lessened for me if I had understood that the anonymity Tradition applies at the public level and not the private. I grin now when I hear someone say that he broke his anonymity by telling his grandmother he was in AA. We understand one another—anonymity and me.

E. S.

# Admirable Simplicity
December 1998

Two things happened recently that made me give a great deal of thought to how the spiritual principle of anonymity can get tangled in very real circumstances.

A few weeks ago I got a call from a friend in the Fellowship who was deeply upset over her anonymity being broken. As an officer of her group, her name and address had been included in the group's listing at our intergroup office and, through a highly unusual series of events, her participation in AA became known to the head of her organization. He called her in and told her that if the fact that she was an alcoholic became known he would have to consider letting her go. She was deeply, and understandably, distressed.

What the event brought home to me was how vital anonymity is, not only as a spiritual asset, but as a practical matter, and that no matter how I myself may choose to govern my own anonymity, protecting others is also my responsibility. I must never be casual about the anonymity of others. Alcoholism can be greatly misunderstood, as I know from my own experience.

I had no idea what being an alcoholic meant until I found I might be one. I had to overcome my own long-standing idea that being alcoholic was both a moral and character defect. Remembering my own prejudices, I don't expect nonalcoholics to understand my disease or believe that being a member of AA is an asset. But no matter what others may believe, anonymity protects me from being misunderstood by those who do not have a life-and-death stake in using AA to stay sober.

When I was newly sober, I honored anonymity out of timidity. I might be an alcoholic, but I didn't want the world to know. I wasn't overjoyed to find I'd nearly ruined and lost my life through drinking.

As I got past shame, I began to understand the true importance of anonymity, trusting the idea that I should be the only copy of the Big Book someone might read. My actions should serve as my message.

Early on, the two times I broke my anonymity because I was determined to "do good," the efforts came to nothing, my target's expressions clearly telling me to mind my own business. They were right, because I'd let my will govern my instincts. Since then, every time I've broken my anonymity, it has been the result of some inner prompting that has taken me, and the hearer, completely by surprise. I remember that, as I told someone about my drinking life and finding help in AA, I found myself thinking, Why in the world are you telling him all this? As it turned out, he needed to know. That impulse to speak has always led to a good result. Much to my surprise, those I've told have gotten and stayed sober, and I have the relief of knowing how very little it had to do with me.

Waiting for that inner prompting to move me to action helps keep me right-sized and honors the simple and clear intention of the Step: I have a duty to carry the message, but I'm also well-advised to honor the spiritual power of anonymity. I may know who needs the message, but I'll probably never be sure who's ready to hear it or that I'm the one who can best carry it. And that brings me to the second recent event.

I had a call from a sponsee who spends weekends at a beach house in a small vacation community where AA has become a strong presence. He'd been asked by a fellow member to go on an unasked-for call on a woman in the community who was in very obvious trouble with drinking. He and his friend planned to go to the woman and tell her they were in AA and say it was apparent that she needed AA's help. A recent trip to a rehab hadn't convinced her. He wanted to know what I thought.

I don't like telling my sponsees what to do, preferring to see if I can help them see for themselves what might be best. I hemmed and hawed, until it finally struck me that this was an unusually clear-cut case. I told him I thought it was a bad, if not a terrible, idea. He would probably be doing the unwanted for the unwilling, and he should trust that when and if she was ever ready, the need and usefulness of AA would become abundantly clear. As a practical matter, he saw a fair amount of the woman and what was intended as a bridge might well have become a barrier if she chose to avoid him.

In my own case, if someone had told me a second before I was ready to hear it that the greatest love of my life was a sly and destructive villain, I would have been furious and my resistance to AA's message would have hardened. From what I hear at meetings, it seems that most of us are surprised into sobriety.

Anonymity is a powerfully practical spiritual tool that I break only when moved to. I don't have to figure it out. I don't have to decide who needs to hear the message and that I'm a member of AA. Otherwise, I might be the wrong messenger speaking in a way that either makes no sense or alienates the hearer.

The first year I was sober I attended New York's annual Bill W. Dinner and heard his wife Lois read Bill's last message to the assembly, as she did annually, as long as she was able. When Bill W. wrote that message, he knew he was gravely ill and chose, above all other matters he might have spoken of, to emphasize the vital importance of anonymity. As the years have gone by, his message grows clearer to me and I'm more and more struck by the practical sanity of both the Steps and Traditions. Even if there weren't a powerful spiritual component to them, they would serve remarkably well as common-sense bulwarks against AA losing its power to help people like me.

Tradition Twelve sets out what's required with admirable simplicity and seems to work best when I put that principle ahead of my personality.

Bob R.
New York, New York

# Good for Nothing
January 1989
(From *Dear Grapevine*)

L iving the Twelfth Tradition is a lesson in humility when applied on an individual basis. It prohibits me from upstaging AA and keeps the spotlight off of myself. It keeps me from calling up political and religious leaders and telling them a thing or two. It keeps still my pen when a psychiatrist decides that AA needs to be controlled. You see, my personality still gets me in trouble, but not like it did before sobriety.

Anonymity keeps my name and picture completely out of the media. It protects me from myself. But there is another side to this beautiful word, and I rarely ever hear it discussed at meetings. Anonymity means to do something for somebody else and keep my big mouth shut, not even letting the person on the receiving end know who the giver is. Now that, my dear friends, leads to spiritual growth in the area of humility. A man with a lot of years in AA coined a phrase for it: Being good for nothing. Try it, you'll like it.

Anonymous
Shreveport, Louisiana

# Our Protective Mantle
December 1992

M y thoughts about anonymity have usually emphasized its therapeutic value in controlling such psychological handicaps as egotism and greed. I have occasionally been surprised to find that in the minds of many members of Alcoholics Anonymous the chief function of anonymity—nay, its only purpose—is to conceal and protect its members.

If I am reasonably sure that they will not broadcast the information to the media in violation of our Traditions, I have told the people I mingle with frequently that I belong to Alcoholics Anonymous. Recently one of these people was drawn into the counseling sessions of an alcohol-abuse treatment program for a family member. She talked to me rather freely about her reactions to what went on in group therapy at the hospital.

I was interested in the reactions of my nonalcoholic, intelligent, and only minimally neurotic friend to the kind of psychological therapy being administered to her relative. I had missed getting any professional help by simply plunking myself down in an AA meeting and not taking the first drink.

She had naively assumed that because I was an ardent AA member, and since the treatment center, they said, was AA-oriented, I must be familiar with the type of emotional and mental education going on there. She mentioned confrontations, for instance, where you come right out and tell your loved ones—in front of other people!—how they have really made you feel. I had to admit to her that I have, once or twice in small meetings, witnessed somebody break down and tearfully or angrily tell somebody else off. But ordinarily we AAs just sit there with calm but intent faces, listening without interruption to whatever wisdom or nonsense a given speaker is lavishing upon us.

One day my friend burst out, "How do you deal with this 'no secrets business?'" I had to ask her what she meant.

"Oh, you know, all this 'You can't have secrets. You have to come out with everything.'"

"In Alcoholics Anonymous," I said, "I've never had to deal with anything like that."

"Don't you have to get up and tell all—about what you did when you were drinking?"

I laughed. "Not all, if I don't care to. In fact, not anything—if I don't want to. Only what I'm ready to tell, when I'm ready."

"What about that Fifth Step—and admitting to yourselves, to God, and to another human being the exact nature of your wrongs?"

"It doesn't say anything about a whole bunch of human beings. Of course, if you like spilling your guts to an audience, it's OK. We'll listen, probably with avid fascination. But the 'other human being' can be anybody you choose, even someone you will never see again."

My friend's resentment of this "no secrets" approach lingered in the wings of the stage that is my mind until one day it connected in a flare of recognition with what I knew about the reasons for our becoming anonymous in the first place. It was worse 57 years ago when Bill and Bob started AA; but even now the people who come to us for help are ashamed, afraid, asking the same old questions: How could this have happened to me? What must other people think of me?

Today, as then, we invite those newcomers to crawl under the warm tent of anonymity with us where they can be seen only by the eyes of those who have felt the same incomprehensible demoralization that they are feeling. We don't even ask their names. If they wish, they can make one up, just so we'll have something to call them by.

Most of us are basically courteous people. In my 25-plus years in AA I have rarely had my privacy violated. We seem to know by instinct that prying into one another's personal lives is taboo. We accept that if you want us to learn more of the details of your private affairs you will tell us.

It can be a matter of days, weeks, months or even years before we divulge our surnames, addresses, job status or family affiliations. If there are facts about yourself which you deliberately keep "secret," nobody in AA really cares. That's your business.

And it's better that way. With all your secrets safely shrouded in anonymity, we get to know who you really are—aside from your worldly accomplishments or failures, your financial status, your checkered past. We get a chance to get acquainted with what, for lack of a better word, I'll call your soul.

Let us guard against too much leakage in our protective covering of anonymity. There are only two words in the name of this Fellowship to which we belong. The second word, "anonymous," defines us. No other method of treatment for our disease uses this rigorous discipline. It is part of what gets and keeps us well. Please don't play fast and loose with this magnificent weapon against our disease.

Bernice M.
Los Gatos, California

————————◆————————

# THE TWELVE STEPS

1. We admitted we were powerless over alcohol—that our lives had become unmanageable.
2. Came to believe that a Power greater than ourselves could restore us to sanity.
3. Made a decision to turn our will and our lives over to the care of God *as we understood Him*.
4. Made a searching and fearless moral inventory of ourselves.
5. Admitted to God, to ourselves, and to another human being the exact nature of our wrongs.
6. Were entirely ready to have God remove all these defects of character.
7. Humbly asked Him to remove our shortcomings.
8. Made a list of all persons we had harmed, and became willing to make amends to them all.
9. Made direct amends to such people wherever possible, except when to do so would injure them or others.
10. Continued to take personal inventory and when we were wrong promptly admitted it.
11. Sought through prayer and meditation to improve our conscious contact with God *as we understood Him*, praying only for knowledge of His will for us and the power to carry that out.
12. Having had a spiritual awakening as the result of these steps, we tried to carry this message to alcoholics, and to practice these principles in all our affairs.

# THE TWELVE TRADITIONS

1. Our common welfare should come first; personal recovery depends upon A.A. unity.
2. For our group purpose there is but one ultimate authority—a loving God as He may express Himself in our group conscience. Our leaders are but trusted servants; they do not govern.
3. The only requirement for A.A. membership is a desire to stop drinking.
4. Each group should be autonomous except in matters affecting other groups or A.A. as a whole.
5. Each group has but one primary purpose—to carry its message to the alcoholic who still suffers.
6. An A.A. group ought never endorse, finance or lend the A.A. name to any related facility or outside enterprise, lest problems of money, property and prestige divert us from our primary purpose.
7. Every A.A. group ought to be fully self-supporting, declining outside contributions.
8. Alcoholics Anonymous should remain forever nonprofessional, but our service centers may employ special workers.
9. A.A., as such, ought never be organized; but we may create service boards or committees directly responsible to those they serve.
10. Alcoholics Anonymous has no opinion on outside issues; hence the A.A. name ought never be drawn into public controversy.
11. Our public relations policy is based on attraction rather than promotion; we need always maintain personal anonymity at the level of press, radio and films.
12. Anonymity is the spiritual foundation of all our traditions, ever reminding us to place principles before personalities.

# Alcoholics Anonymous

AA's program of recovery is fully set forth in its basic text, *Alcoholics Anonymous* (commonly known as the Big Book), now in its Fourth Edition, as well as in *Twelve Steps and Twelve Traditions, Living Sober,* and other books. Information on AA can also be found on AA's website at WWW.AA.ORG, or by writing to:

Alcoholics Anonymous
Box 459
Grand Central Station
New York, NY 10163

For local resources, check your local telephone directory under "Alcoholics Anonymous." Four pamphlets, "This is A.A.," "Is A.A. For You?," "44 Questions," and "A Newcomer Asks" are also available from AA.

# AA Grapevine

AA Grapevine is AA's international monthly journal, published continuously since its first issue in June 1944. The AA pamphlet on AA Grapevine describes its scope and purpose this way: "As an integral part of Alcoholics Anonymous since 1944, the Grapevine publishes articles that reflect the full diversity of experience and thought found within the A.A. Fellowship, as does La Viña, the bimonthly Spanish-language magazine, first published in 1996. No one viewpoint or philosophy dominates their pages, and in determining content, the editorial staff relies on the principles of the Twelve Traditions."

In addition to magazines, AA Grapevine, Inc. also produces books, eBooks, audiobooks, and other items. It also offers a Grapevine Online subscription, which includes: four new stories monthly, AudioGrapevine (the audio version of the magazine), Grapevine Story Archive (the entire collection of Grapevine articles), and the current issue of Grapevine and La Viña in HTML format. For more information on AA Grapevine, or to subscribe to any of these, please visit the magazine's website at WWW.AAGRAPEVINE.ORG or write to:

AA Grapevine, Inc.
475 Riverside Drive
New York, NY 10115